A BROWN PAPER SCHOOL BOOK

Making Cents

Every Kid's Guide to Money
How to Make It, What to Do with It

by Elizabeth Wilkinson

drawings by Martha Weston

Little, Brown and Company

Boston   Toronto   London

A YOLLA BOLLY PRESS BOOK

This Brown Paper School book was edited and prepared for publication at The Yolla Bolly Press, Covelo, California. The series is under the supervision of James and Carolyn Robertson. Editorial and production staff: Barbara Youngblood, Nancy Campbell, Diana Fairbanks.

This book is based on *Good Cents* published by Houghton Mifflin in 1974.

Library of Congress Cataloging-in-Publication Data

Wilkinson, Elizabeth, 1926–
    Making cents: every kid's guide to money/by Elizabeth Wilkinson; illustrated by Martha Weston.
        p.cm. — (A Brown paper school book)
    Summary: Explores the concept of money and illustrates several ways to earn money.
    ISBN 0-316-94101-8
    ISBN 0-316-94102-6 (pbk.)
    1. Moneymaking projects for children—Juvenile literature.   2. Success in business—Juvenile literature. 3. Finance, Personal—Juvenile literature. 4. Money—Juvenile literature.
    [1. Moneymaking projects.   2. Finance, Personal. 3. Money.]
    I. Weston, Martha, ill.   II. Title.
    HD2341.W48   1989
    332.024—dc19   88-34634
                                                            CIP
                                                            AC

ISBN: 0-316-94101-8
        0-316-94102-6 (pbk)

HC: 10   9   8   7   6   5   4   3   2   1
PB: 10   9   8   7   6   5   4   3   2   1

*Published simultaneously in Canada
by Little, Brown & Company (Canada) Limited*

PRINTED IN THE UNITED STATES OF AMERICA

95-1155

Table of Contents

PREFACE

This book is about what kids can do to make money in their spare time. There are really only two basic ways to earn money. One is to make or gather something that someone else is willing to buy. The other is to do some task that someone else is willing to pay you for doing. Since spare time can be anything from a few hours to a weekend to every minute you can take off from school and chores for several weeks or months, we have included ideas for a wide variety of projects, crafts, and services. Some of them take a good deal of time and on-going effort. Others are accomplished in a few hours or days. Before you decide to launch yourself into business you should decide just how much time and effort you want to put into "making money."

This book is not just about the jobs kids can do to earn money but, more important, about how they can have a good time doing it. Some people think that a job or working automatically means doing things that you don't enjoy, things like emptying the garbage or washing dishes. Of course, those jobs have to be done, and it's only fair that we all take turns doing them, but there are other kinds of work that are interesting and, yes, fun.

The luckiest people in the world are the ones who earn money doing the things they love to do. They would rather spend their time working than. . . . I started to say, "than playing," but it occurred to me that those are just words, "working" and "playing." What seems like work to one person may be the most enjoyable form of play to another. While we're on the subject of working and playing and having fun, think about the things

5

that you really enjoy doing. They are usually the things that you do well. If you are good at baseball or drawing or playing chess, it's probably because you have spent a great deal of time and energy developing your skills. The same thing is true of work: It's only fun if you take it seriously and are willing to put a lot of effort into doing the best job you can.

The important things to remember when you are deciding on a way to earn money is that it be something that you truely like to do, and that it will not conflict with school or home commitments. Don't decide to deliver papers just because your older brother used to do it. Do it because you like to get up early and ride around the neighborhood in the cool, quiet dawn hours. Think carefully about what things you enjoy and what you don't enjoy. We are all different and need different things to make us comfortable and happy. Some people like to be by themselves or with only one close friend, others love to be in the center of a crowd. You may be the type of person who needs to be doing something active and energetic or you may just prefer to sit and do some quiet project. Think about these things when you are deciding on what sort of a job you would like. Remember, too, that we all change as we grow. What interests you at one time may seem a dead bore at another, so keep an open mind. The experiments you make with jobs when you're young may be a great help later when you are deciding what you want to do as an adult. When you use this book don't feel that you have

to follow our plans or ideas right down to the last detail. Everyone has their own special style that's right for them, and you are the only one who can decide what it is. This is what makes writing a book about ways for kids to earn money so interesting, trying to imagine all the different kinds of people you are, and the different talents you have, and the hundreds of possibilities there are for you to use those talents for fun and maybe a little profit.

The last few pages of this book look quite different from the rest. There are fewer drawings and no ideas for making money, but you will find them interesting just the same. In the Green Pages, you will learn about banks and savings and loan associations, and how and why people put their money in one or the other. There is information about income taxes, Social Security cards, licenses, and permits—things that you probably won't have to deal with until you're a grown-up, but important things to know. The Green Pages also talk about some things that will be very interesting to you right now! For instance, how to keep track of the money you earn, and, if you have partners in your business, how to make sure everyone gets his or her fair share of the profits. You will learn how to make change without getting confused, and how to decide what business to go into in the first place. The most important part of the Green Pages is the suggestion of things you can do to make your customers happy and ensure that they will return to your business again and again.

ANYTIMERS

Adrienne's I-Love-Animals Factory

Adrienne is twelve, and she has been making animal drawings and stuffed animals since she was ten. This year she decided to make big, stuffed-animal pillows and sell them in a store. Everyone liked them, and she sold all she made. Here is what she did.

First, she made some big drawings on paper to help her decide about colors and shapes. Then she cut fabric into the animal shape. She folded the fabric double and pinned her drawing to it. Then she cut out two pieces the right shape, so she had a front and a back for her animal. But she didn't cut it exactly the same size as her drawing; she added about ¾ inch all the way around to allow for seams.

Adrienne put the front and back together with the right sides of the fabric facing each other on the inside and sewed it all around except for one place that she left open so she could stuff it. When

7

it was sewed, she turned it right side out so the seam was on the inside.

Then she stuffed the pillow with shredded foam rubber. You can use the stuffing from an old pillow, or buy polyester filling at a fabric store.

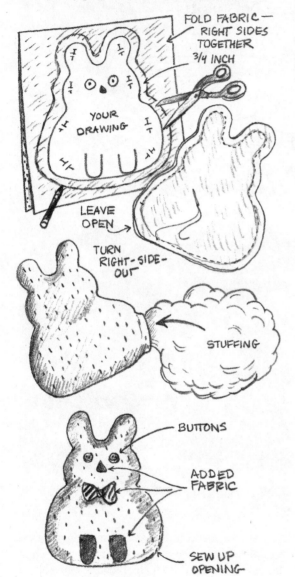

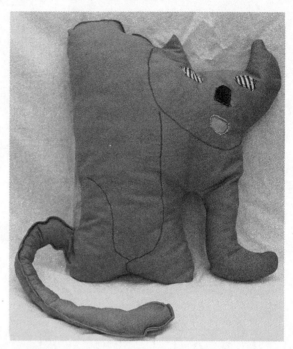

Adrienne works pretty fast. She designed her first three animal pillows one night and made them all one Saturday. She sold the two little ones for $3.50 and the big one for $5.00.

If you like to sew and can get fabric scraps and a sewing machine from someone, you can have a lot of fun inventing animals and bringing them to life.

You can sell your pillows to your parents' friends, or you can sell them in stores. If you sell them in a store, the store will add its own share to what it pays you, and sell the pillows for more. This is how stores make money. For example, the store pays you $2.50 for a small pillow and sells the pillow for $5.00 or more. So if you sell to a store, you may have to sell the pillow for a lower price. But that's okay because a store will usually buy more than one at a time.

When Adrienne was all done, she made tags for each of her animals. One looked like this.

Last, Adrienne sewed up the small opening and sewed on the decorations. On some animals she made the eyes and mouths by sewing on fabrics of different colors; on others she used buttons. Skinny tails and ears can be made by turning in the hems and sewing them on top (topstitching) so they don't have to be turned inside out. Then they can be stuffed and attached to the finished animal at the end.

CRIMSTON
A GReen MAGICAL CAT
He's nice to be around when
there's no-one else around
Also Arfy a bear and Smack a Mouserab

The Hand-and-Foot Printer

You already know what a printer does, but did you know that there are lots of kids who have their own printing presses in their basements (or attics or garages) and who make their own spending money by printing things for people? Did you know that you can start a printing shop without having to buy a real printing press or type or other tools that cost a lot of money? Well, you can, and here's how to start the Potato Press.

You Will Need
    some large potatoes
    small tubes of water-based block-
      printing ink
    a paring or x-acto knife
    an ink roller
    a piece of waxed paper

First, make a design on paper. Make a small, simple one because you are going to carve it into the potato. Solid shapes work best. Cut the potato into two or three chunks. Copy the design by scratching the shape lightly into one of the cut ends. Now, by cutting down about ⅛ to ¼ inch, carefully cut away the surface of the potato that is not part of your design. The rest of the potato is your "handle."

Squeeze a dab of ink the size of a big pea onto a piece of waxed paper. Roll it out a bit with your ink roller to form a thin film. You can use your finger to do this if you don't have a roller. Press the potato gently into the ink two or three times to make sure the raised design is completely covered. Now press the potato firmly *straight down* onto a piece of smooth paper. And there you have it.

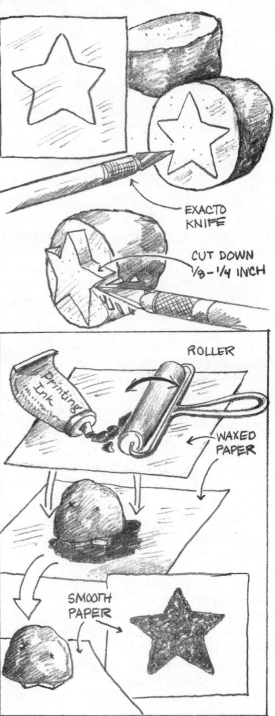

EXACTO KNIFE

CUT DOWN ⅛–¼ INCH

ROLLER

Printing Ink

WAXED PAPER

SMOOTH PAPER

When you are making a cardboard printer, instead of cutting the background away, you are building up the images with layers of cardboard shapes. To start, decide what size you want your finished print to be and cut a piece of cardboard to the exact size, or slightly smaller if you want a plain border. Draw your design on a piece of paper and transfer it to another piece of light cardboard (like the kind that comes from the laundry in men's shirts). Cut out the basic shapes with scissors and glue them in place on the background cardboard. Now you can add details with a third and even a fourth layer of cardboard cutouts. Allow the glue to dry thoroughly before inking your cardboard printer.

Things You Can Make with a Potato Press

A potato press is just right for making small sheets of wrapping paper for small packages. Buy a roll of plain white shelf paper from the grocery store. (Be sure to get the paper kind, not the plastic-coated stuff.) You can cut this paper into sheets and print them with potato stamps in many patterns and colors. Sell ten sheets for $1.00. Be sure to include with the ten sheets ten tiny gift cards made with the same potato stamps.

You can make stationery for your friends. Cut their initials or their favorite designs into the potato. If you cut letter shapes, be sure to cut them *backward* into the potato, so they will read *frontward* when you print them. Print ten plain sheets of dime-store writing paper and ten envelopes for $1.00 or more, depending on the cost of the paper.

The Cardboard Press

If you want to make larger, more complicated designs than will fit on a potato, try a cardboard printer. They're not as good for making wrapping paper, but they are great for making greeting cards.

You Will Need
lightweight cardboard
scissors
white glue
tubes of water-soluble printing ink
a rubber ink roller
a piece of window glass or plastic to
    roll it on

YOUR DRAWING

THIN CARD-BOARD

BACKGROUND CARDBOARD

WHITE GLUE

Squeeze some ink out on the sheet of glass and roll it out until the roller is covered with a thin film of ink, then roll it onto the cardboard printer. Some ink will get on the background, but most will adhere to the raised parts. Don't worry; it won't spoil the print.

ROLL IN ALL DIRECTIONS FOR EVEN INK COATING

You may lay the paper on top of the cardboard printer and gently rub it with the bowl of a spoon, or you may put the printer face down on the paper and press from above. Make several test prints to see how you like your design. Try using two blending colors of ink, like red and yellow or blue and green. Roll the printer once with yellow and then again lightly with red. If you want to add something to your print, just let the cardboard dry and glue on some new details.

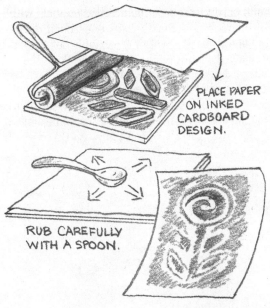

PLACE PAPER ON INKED CARDBOARD DESIGN.

RUB CAREFULLY WITH A SPOON.

The Linoleum Press

If you have tried potato and cardboad printing and want to go on to something more complicated, then you should try printing from linoleum blocks. These are more expensive and harder to cut, but they're worth the extra cost and effort.

You Will Need
    carbon paper
    linoleum blocks (buy them already made at the art store, or make them yourself)
    a set of linoleum-cutting tools
    ink
    a rubber ink roller
    a pane of glass

If you want to make your own linoleum blocks, go to a floor-covering store that carries heavy commercial linoleum. Ask the shop owner if he has any scraps you can have or if you can buy a small piece. Glue the linoleum to squares of smooth wood, about ⅝ to ¾ inches thick.

Cut the block about the same way you did the potato. You'll soon discover that you can get many more fine details on a linoleum block. You can trace your design directly onto the block with carbon paper. *Remember: If you have words in your design, they have to be cut backward in order to print frontward.*

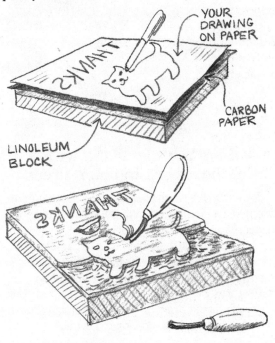

YOUR DRAWING ON PAPER

CARBON PAPER

LINOLEUM BLOCK

11

When the block is cut, ink it with the roller, as you did with your cardboard printer. Lay the paper on the inked block. There are a couple of ways to make the print.

1. You can rub it all over with the bottom of a tablespoon. This is good for blocks that aren't too big. Be sure to press down firmly and to rub all parts of the block to transfer all the ink to the paper.

2. You can stomp it with tennis shoes on. If you try this method, cover the back of the paper with a piece of cardboard and step down straight so that the paper can't twist and smear the print. Gently put all your weight on the foot that is on the block, then move your foot to another part of the block and repeat. Be sure to step all over the block. Ths method is best for big blocks with large solid areas.

① CARDBOARD
② PAPER
Don't wiggle!
③ CUT AND INKED LINOLEUM BLOCK
STEP DOWN STRAIGHT

Things You Can Make with a Cardboard or Linoleum Press

You can make small posters, the kind that fit on telephone poles or on bulletin boards in public places. You can make neat Christmas or gift cards. If you want them to look very professional, ask a printer to get some blank cards with matching envelopes for you. (Some stationery and variety stores carry them too.) Choose four of your very best designs and print up a batch of cards in four different colors. Package them in sets of twenty (five of each design) with envelopes. Sandwich bags make good, neat packages. Sell them for $2.00 to $3.00, depending on how much you had to pay for the paper.

Linoleum and cardboard prints are just right for making bookplates. A bookplate is a label that you paste inside the cover of a book to tell to whom the book belongs. They usually have a design and a place where you can write the owner's name. They can be printed on any kind of lightweight paper. Package them thirty to a bag. Take some to the local bookstore and ask the owner if he or she would sell them for you. Charge $3.00 per package. Tell the bookshop owner to keep $1.00 for each package sold; you will earn $2.00 for each package. Make a sign saying that you will take special orders to make personalized bookplates with the owner's name printed on them. Then all you need to do is make a separate block for the customer's name. Charge $4.00 to $5.00 for these.

RUTH YOUNG

After you have fooled around with potato prints and cardboard and linoleum blocks and saved up some money, you can expand your print shop by buying a real printing press. If you live in a city and watch the classified ads under "Machinery" and "Office Equipment" and "Miscellaneous," you can sometimes find printing presses for sale. Even a small used press can cost a lot of money, and you'll need other tools as well, so don't plan to get a press until you've tried the other kinds of printing first.

Kids
for
Art

You may not know this, but lots of grown-ups are cuckoo about kids' artwork. I don't know why. Maybe it's because most kids aren't afraid to draw and paint, and grown-ups wish they were like that too. Here is a way you can make some money and have a lot of fun by making art shows for grown-ups. You and your friends can start a Kids' Art Company. Your company can make shows to go wherever there are empty, boring walls to look at.

Think about all the places people have to be for hours or all day with nothing cheerful to look at. Places like hospitals and nursing homes, train and bus stations, doctors' and dentists' offices. Other places that may be interested in a kids' art exhibit are public libraries and recreation centers. Take some of your best drawings or paintings to the people in charge of these places. Tell them that you can bring a bright and colorful show of ten pieces of kids' art for a month for only $5.00. Tell the person in charge that he or she can sell each painting for $1.00 and keep half of the money. (That way the show doesn't cost anything for the month, and you could earn extra money.) Here's how that works. When you put up the show, charge $5.00. After one month, come back. Take away the art that wasn't sold. Collect half the money for the art that was sold. If the whole show was sold ($1.00 × 10 paintings = $10.00), your customer keeps $5.00 and you collect $5.00.

Be sure the drawings and paintings are your very best ones. People can tell if you whip up a batch of things just to make a show. Choose carefully. Make sure there is a mixture of sizes and colors. Most important, be sure you figure out a way to display your drawings and paintings that makes them look their best. Each one should be glued or fastened to something that can be hung on the wall and that looks nice. Be sure each piece has the artist's name on it.

THESE PICTURES WERE MADE BY BIN WONG, 11 SALENE HILL, 12 AND NANCY ADAMS, 9½ THEY ARE FOR SALE FOR $1.00 EACH

Getting Your Show Ready

This is important: Near where the show is hanging, there should be a sign that explains where it came from. You might make one that says something like this:

THESE PAINTINGS WERE PUT HERE BY
KIDS
TO CHEER YOU UP.
***** THEY ARE FOR SALE *****
FOR $1.00 EACH.
PLEASE ASK IF YOU WANT TO BUY
ONE.

Here are two ways to get your drawings and paintings ready to hang in the art show. The getting ready is a very important part of your business. It should be done carefully.

If the painting can be cut smaller without hurting it, fold it over a piece of corrugated cardboard at least an inch smaller on all sides than your painting and glue it down with white glue. Wrap the whole thing smoothly with clear plastic wrap and tape it firmly together on the back. Cover the back with a piece of paper the same size as the cardboard and glue it down. Glue a picture hook on the back near the top.

If the picture shouldn't be cut down to a smaller size, cut out a piece of cardboard 3 or 4 inches longer and wider than your drawing. Paint one side of the cardboard with white glue, slightly thinned with water. Place the cardboard, glue side down, on a piece of fairly thin fabric that's at least one inch larger all the way around. The fabric should be a plain color that complements the picture. Paint glue on the excess fabric and fold it neatly over the back of the cardboard. When the glue is dry, tack your painting on the cardboard mat with straight pins, pushed in at an angle. Glue a picture hook on the back, or attach stick-on picture hangers and string.

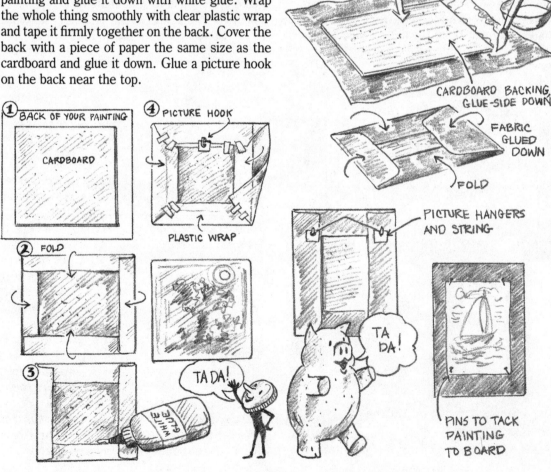

14

The Computer Kid

Attention, eggheads! Do you like working with a computer? Do you have one at home that you can use whenever you want to? Well, put your know-how and your computer to work. Think about some of the things that a computer does easily, like making multiple copies. It's great for jobs where you need to update printed information on a regular basis. Now think of all the jobs that you and your computer could do to help other people and to earn some pocket money for you.

Go to the local restaurants and offer to print up menus for them. Check out the restaurants ahead of time so you'll know what kind of menus they use. Some restaurants change their menus every day, others will need notices only of their daily specials. Have several samples of similar menus to show them. Make the menus look more decorative with headings and footings made with rows of standard typewriter symbols like these:

```
****************************************
%%%%%%%%%%%%%%%%%%%%%%%%%
= = = = = = = = = = = = = = = = = = = =
##########################
=!=!=!=!=!=!=!=!=!=!=!=!=!=!
@@@@@@@@@@@@@@@@@@@@@@@
+ + + + + + + + + + + + + + + + + + + +
( = )( = )( = )( = )( = )( = )( = )( = )( = )( = )( = )( = )
!!!!!!!!!!!!!!!!!!!!!!!!!!!!!!!!!!!!!!!!!!!!!!!!!!!!!!!!!!!!!!
```

YOUR SAMPLE MENUS

A RESTAURANT MANAGER OR OWNER

If you're a pretty good typist and are careful about your spelling, you could get jobs printing up newsletters for organizations or people who send out announcements or information bulletins from time to time.

After you have done some jobs with the word processor and have made some money, you might go shopping for a program that does pictures and expand your business. With graphics programs you can do all sorts of decorative printing, such as personalized greeting cards, diplomas, awards, announcements, invitations, signs, and bookplates. Some computers will print in color, but even if yours will print only in black ink, you can buy computer paper in bright colors and create wonderful effects.

You can make neat banners with these types of programs too, ones that say things like HAPPY BIRTHDAY, GLORIA! or GET WELL SOON, PETER, or WELCOME HOME, PATTY! or I LOVE YOU, ALLISON—WILL YOU MARRY ME?

Where to Look for Business

For printing jobs, you will just have to go out and look for business. Here are some ideas of people to ask and places to go: retirement homes, social organizations, small businesses, health clubs, garden clubs, dance groups, churches, music teachers, language teachers, tutors. When you get a job, find out all the particulars and write them down. Find out how many copies will be needed, what day they are needed, and how many days ahead of time you can pick up the copy. What you charge will depend on the length of the printing and the number of copies needed. Don't forget to figure in the cost of the paper.

Take some samples of your personalized greeting cards and banners to the local gift shop or variety store. Tell the storekeeper that you will make up special orders and if he or she sells them for you, the store can keep part of the money. Work out your prices with the storekeeper.

15

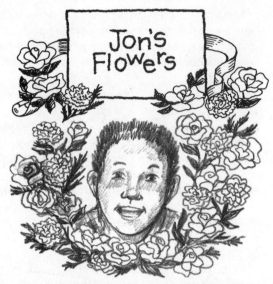

Jon's Flowers

Once upon a time there was a kid named Jon who figured out a great way to make people happy on special celebration days, and how to make some money for himself by doing it. He would phone the husbands in his neighborhood when their wives weren't home. He'd say something like this:

> Hello, Mr. Finster, this is Jon Wilson. I'm selling a flower service for birthdays and anniversaries. If you place an order now, I'll see that the flowers are delivered on the right day, or you can pick them up at my house if you want to make sure they're a surprise.
>
> I can get you a dozen roses from the Chelsea Flower Shop for x amount or a dozen carnations for y amount.

Then the husband might say:

> Great! I can surprise my wife and not have to bother getting the flowers from the florist myself, and I won't have to take a chance on forgetting at the last minute.

Jon talked to different flower shops ahead of time to find one that would agree to his project. He got prices for several different kinds of flowers. Then he added $2.00 to the price for his service. He also found out how far in advance the flower shop needed his order.

This worked so well that he did the same thing at Christmastime with wreaths and poinsettias. His business was a little easier at Christmastime because it wasn't a surprise and he could take orders door-to-door.

If you think this would be a good project for you, you might consider doing it at Valentine's Day or Easter. Just be sure to start making your phone calls well before the holiday. Take careful notes during your phone calls and get in the habit of recording on a calendar the day you should place the order and the day it should be delivered or picked up. Be sure that you check your calendar every day. If you mess up and forget a delivery, it could make someone pretty unhappy.

Start Your Own Neighborhood Nursery

Here's how to grow and sell indoor plants. If you like to make things grow, it could be a fine after-school business. Most people don't take the trouble to start their own plants. If yours are healthy and not too expensive, you will have no trouble selling them. You can include instructions for watering and other care. Charge 50¢ for small plants and up to $2.00 for larger ones or ones with blooms.

How Much Can You Make?

Income from selling 80 plants
   at 50¢ each $40.00
Cost of soil $7.00
Cost of Rootone 5.00
What you spend 12.00
What you make. $28.00

Here is what you will need to start your own neighborhood nursery.

1. Cuttings. You get these starts from plants that are already growing.

2. Soil. If you live in the city, you may have to buy potting soil. Actually, it's probably a good idea anyway. For one thing, it has been sterilized, so you won't be bothered by weeds, and it's lighter and richer in humus than most garden soil. A bag containing 2 cubic feet, enough for 80 plants, costs about $7.00.

3. Containers. Any small container, like cut-off milk cartons or small tin cans. Don't buy them. Find them.

4. A growing place. Could be any sheltered place that has good light and isn't too cold: a windowsill, an enclosed porch, a fire escape or balcony, or a table by a window.

5. Root hormone. Roots will grow from cuttings without it, but it helps plants get a good start. You can buy a package of Rootone for about $5.00, and that's enough for about 100 plants.

6. Time. It will take anywhere from three weeks to six weeks for cuttings to root and get big and strong enough to sell.

Some Plants to Try

All of these plants are easy to propagate without any fancy equipment or a whole lot of care. We've given you their Latin names as well as their common names. If you want to find out more about them from a garden book, look in the index for their Latin names. Sometimes the same common name is used for several different plants, and it's very confusing.

This is how they look full grown.

WANDERING JEW. *TRADESCANTIA FLUMINENSIS.* THIS PLANT IS GREAT FOR HANGING, AND IT GROWS FAST. THE ONES WITH STRIPED LEAVES NEED LOTS OF SUN. START FROM CUTTINGS ROOTED IN WATER.

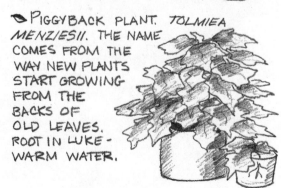

PIGGYBACK PLANT. *TOLMIEA MENZIESII.* THE NAME COMES FROM THE WAY NEW PLANTS START GROWING FROM THE BACKS OF OLD LEAVES. ROOT IN LUKE-WARM WATER.

SPIDER PLANT. *CHLOROPHYTUM ELATUM.* THIS IS ANOTHER GOOD PLANT FOR HANGING. IT SENDS OUT MINIATURE SPIDER PLANTS ON LONG DROOPING BRANCHES. THE BABY SPIDERS CAN BE CUT OFF AND WILL ROOT IN WATER IN ABOUT A WEEK.

Here are a few popular flowering plants. Either keep them until they bloom, or tell the new owners the color of the blossoms on the parent plant.

AFRICAN VIOLETS. *SAINT PAULIA IONANTHA.* THESE BEAUTIFUL FLOWERING HOUSEPLANTS ARE VERY EASY TO PROPAGATE. YOU CAN DIVIDE A LARGE, WELL-GROWN PLANT AND REPOT THE DIVISIONS, OR YOU CAN START ANY NUMBER OF NEW PLANTS FROM A SINGLE LEAF SET IN WATER.

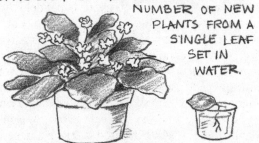

COLEUS. *COLEUS BLUMEI.* THIS PLANT HAS VERY COLORFUL LEAVES. THEY COME IN SHADES OF RED, YELLOW, PURPLE AND GREEN. TIP CUTTINGS WILL ROOT IN WATER OR DIRECTLY IN POTTING SOIL.

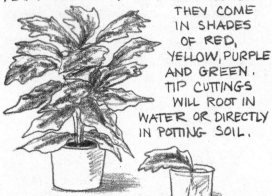

BEGONIAS. *BEGONIA SEMPERFLORENS.* BEGONIAS LIKE THE SHADE, SO GIVE THEM INDIRECT LIGHT. CUTTINGS ROOT IN WATER.

AURORA BOREALIS PLANT. *KALANCHOE BLOSSFELDIANA* OR *K. FEDTSCHENKOI MARGINATA.* KALANCHOE IS AN EXCELLENT HOUSE PLANT WITH CORAL OR RED FLOWERS THAT BLOOM FROM JANUARY THROUGH SPRING. YOU CAN GROW THEM EASILY FROM 4-TO 6-INCH-LONG CUTTINGS PLANTED DIRECTLY IN A MIXTURE OF POTTING SOIL AND SAND.

GRAPE IVY. *CISSUS RHOMBIFOLIA* THIS IS ONE OF THE EASIEST AND PRETTIEST PLANTS FOR HANGING. ROOT CUTTINGS IN WATER AND PLANT IN POTTING SOIL.

Start by taking some cuttings from a big healthy houseplant. You might want to buy some plants to use for parent plants, but you can probably get plenty of cuttings from friends and neighbors. Use sharp scissors or a razor blade to cut off pieces 2 to 3 inches long. Pull off the lower

18

leaves, dip the ends in Rootone, and put them in small jars of lukewarm water.

You can put several cuttings in one jar, but be sure the roots have room to grow without getting tangled. You'll see the roots begin to sprout in a few days. Some plants take longer to root than others, and a lot depends on how much heat and light they get. Don't put them in direct sun. Check them every day to make sure there is enough water in the jar. In about two weeks (for most plants), or when the roots are about 2 inches long, plant your cuttings in potting soil. First, fill your containers with potting soil. Then, to avoid damaging the roots, make a small hole with a pencil, place the cutting in the hole, and gently press the soil around it. Water the cutting until the soil is just moist. Don't drown it. Some people give the newly planted cuttings a dose of vitamin B_1 to reduce the shock. Make a little greenhouse for your plants by setting them in a plastic bag. Leave the bag slightly open at the top for air. Open the bag a little more every day to allow the plants to harden gradually until they are strong enough to grow in the open.

How to Make Containers

You can make plant containers out of things your mom generally throws away. Small cans, plastic butter tubs, and cut-off milk cartons are all good. Punch holes in the bottoms of the containers with a nail or an ice pick. Make about ten holes in each so that the water will drain out when you water the plants. Since you don't want the water to drain out onto the floor or table, put the containers in a shallow pan. The flat, aluminum roasting pans (the throw-away kind) that you get at the grocery store are good. Put a layer of pebbles in the bottom to raise the containers above the drain-off water.

While you're waiting for your plants to develop roots, spend time getting your containers ready. You'll soon realize that they are a motley-looking bunch and need some fixing up before they go out into the world to be sold. One way to improve the appearance of tin cans or plastic cartons is to paint them. This should be done before planting. Use oil-base paint, ideally the rust-retardant kind. Dull greens or browns or rather gray turquoise blues will make the plants look their best.

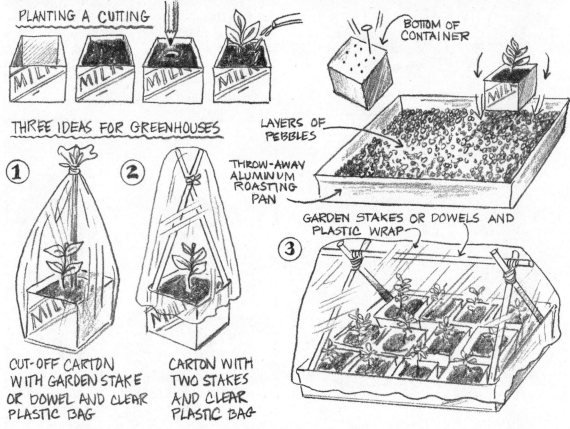

PLANTING A CUTTING

THREE IDEAS FOR GREENHOUSES

① ②

CUT-OFF CARTON WITH GARDEN STAKE OR DOWEL AND CLEAR PLASTIC BAG

CARTON WITH TWO STAKES AND CLEAR PLASTIC BAG

BOTTOM OF CONTAINER

LAYERS OF PEBBLES

THROW-AWAY ALUMINUM ROASTING PAN

GARDEN STAKES OR DOWELS AND PLASTIC WRAP

③

19

You can cover cans or cartons with sticky-backed shelf paper, but avoid bright colors and strong patterns. Or get some of the green waxy paper that florists use to wrap flowers. (Your local florist will probably be happy to sell or even give you some.) Cut it to the right sizes and neatly wrap your containers. This should be done just before you start to sell the plants, otherwise the paper will get dirty and water stained and look worse than the original containers.

Make small cards to go on your plants. Include the common name and the Latin botanical names and the color of the blossom, if any. Give a few tips on care.

How to Sell Your Plants

This will depend on where you live and the time of year. If it's warm enough outside, you might load some of your best plants in a wagon and go door-to-door with them. Or you could set up a display in front of your house. Make a large sign that can be seen from the street, saying:

FINE HEALTHY HOUSEPLANTS
FOR SALE
FROM 50¢
COLEUS WANDERING JEW
GRAPE IVY SPIDER PLANT
PIGGYBACK AFRICAN VIOLETS
BEGONIAS KALANCHOE

In the winter, or if you live in the city in an apartment, you might try making up a flyer to put at people's doors. Tell them what you have to sell and how much you are charging. Give them your telephone number and times when you'll be home to take calls.

The next time there's a flea market or garage sale in your neighborhood, ask if you can show some of your plants. This is a good time to sell the ones that are fancied up to be given as gifts.

If your corner grocery store has space, see if you can display a few plants there. Make up a sign and be sure to tell people that it is a business run by kids. Ask the grocer to sell them for you and let the store keep a third of the money.

SOME OF YOUR PLANTS WILL NEED HANGERS. YOU CAN MAKE GOOD-LOOKING ONES WITH JUST ONE EASY MACRAMÉ KNOT. CHECK YOUR LIBRARY FOR BOOKS ABOUT MACRAMÉ TO FIND A SIMPLE KIND FOR MAKING HANGERS. THIS WOULD BE A GOOD WAY TO SPEND YOUR TIME WHILE WAITING FOR MOTHER NATURE TO MAKE ROOTS. YOU CAN USE ANY STRONG CORD, BUT FUZZY, BROWN JUTE PACKING TWINE LOOKS BEST.

The Hot Fudge Sundae and Other Newspapers

This is a picture of Barb Haines. It was taken when she was in the sixth grade and was coeditor of *The Hot Fudge Sundae*. That's a pretty crazy name for a newspaper. Barb and her friend Nancy Larson used to get together and write up the news and draw the pictures. (It's a lot more fun to do a paper with friends.) They printed their paper by hand, and it was a lot of work. After the pages were done, they tied them with yarn and took the finished papers around to sell. They charged 5¢ each. Here is what *The Hot Fudge Sundae* looked like.

Dear Reader,
White editorials for Big Blob Dean Dill Pickle is open to the public. We would like you to send in stories and poems to Doin Our Own Thing...
and...
to...
or...

HAPPENING (News)

NEW PUPPIES ON BRUCE ST.

Matt Dickerson's dog Ralph just had puppies. There are seven of them. They wer born Thursday July 10 night, and Friday July 11. One is black, 2 are brown and white and 4 are black and white. Matt isn't sure what kind of dogs they are, but they aren't pure breeds.

CARNIVAL TO BE ON BRUCE!

There is going to be a carnival at 837 Bruce (Larsons) It will be at about the end of July or the beginning of August. There will be games, food, rides and the coolest fortune telling. There will be signs up, so don't worry

GO CARTS

Go carts are the new boys on Bruce Street. The present own are Tom Creal, Kevin Terry, and Dickerson. They are made out of wood and are run by lown mower m

Tom Creal

Matt Dickerson

Kevin Terry

THE KNO WHEN POLUT

Graphics Ads

D.B. & B.H.

21

Abigail Brunswitt is in the seventh grade. Her paper is called *The Neighborhood News*. She writes her news on letter-size paper that is folded in half to make pages. Her father takes it to his office, where it is copied on a copy machine. Then Abigail folds and staples the pages and takes them to her subscribers. She sells about fifty papers each time for 20¢ each. Her paper comes out once every two weeks. Sort of. Here are some pages.

You can start your own paper. First, you must like to write stories and make pictures. If you do, and if you have a nose for news, you've got almost everything you need.

Next you need a name. You can call your paper anything you like, but it should be a name that people can remember and one that won't be confused with grown-up papers. It might help to use a name that tells people it's about their neighborhood, like *The Pearl Street Gazette* or *The Sun Valley Neighbor* or *The East Diversey Street Bugle*.

Only you can decide how big to make your paper. Here is some good advice: start small. No one will mind. If you try to make your paper too big, you just might not finish it at all. When you decide on the size paper to use, choose a standard size (that is, one of the standard sizes that paper comes in). Here are two standard sizes: 8½ by 11 and 8½ by 14. Both these sizes go with carbon paper, copy machines, mimeograph machines, and printing presses. Computer paper for word processing comes in one size: an 8½-by-11-inch sheet.

Now you should probably decide how you will print your paper. If you don't know anyone with a copy machine or a mimeograph or a printing press or a computer, then you should start by printing your paper with carbon paper. (It might be a good idea anyway until you've done a few issues and have some experience.) Carbon paper is just a way to make more than one copy when you write the news. You can make five or six copies each time if you press hard. If you want more than five or six copies, you will have to rewrite the whole thing again.

BALLPOINT PEN

You'll get tired of doing the job with carbon paper pretty soon, but by that time you'll know whether you like writing a newspaper and whether your neighbors like reading it. Then it makes sense to expand your business by writing more pages and printing more copies. One way to do this is to take your master copy, all written and illustrated, to someplace where there is a copy machine. Or you can write your news on mimeograph stencils and have them run off in the church or school office, or wherever you can find a mimeograph machine. If you're really lucky, you'll know someone who will let you use her word processor. Then you can write it and print it all in one step. You can leave spaces for illustrations and put those in with carbon paper.

Now you need NEWS. Here is where your imagination is important. Since all the grown-up papers are filled mostly with bad news, maybe your paper should concentrate on telling people mostly good news. (In fact, *Mostly Good News* isn't a bad idea for a paper's name.) Here are some kinds of good news people around your neighborhood might like very much to know about.

How to Get Good News

Every neighborhood is different. You'll have to invent your own methods for getting news, but here are some hints. In every town there are certain people who know lots about what is going on. Get to know who they are and tell them you want their help. Make up some little cards with your phone number that people can tack by their phones. When they find out some good news, they can call you.

Be sure to call every club or organization in your neighborhood. Tell the president of each one that you will print news and notices of club events in your paper. Call them regularly to get their news. Also check with your police and your SPCA for reports of lost items or animals (or found ones). Each week check the school office for news, also the library and all the churches for special events. Soon you'll have more good news than you have space to print.

About Money

A newspaper won't make much money at first. But if you keep it going and people find out about it from their friends and get used to reading it, you will be able to sell more copies and make more money. Don't take money in advance; it's better to sell each issue as you deliver it.

After you have been in business a while and have a lot of subscribers, you can try to sell small ads to local merchants. Advertising space in newspapers is sold by the inch, or by the piece of the page. Make up a price sheet that shows your rates. Keep your prices low. A dollar for one-half or one-third of a page is probably as much as you should ever charge.

23

Mother Nature Card Company

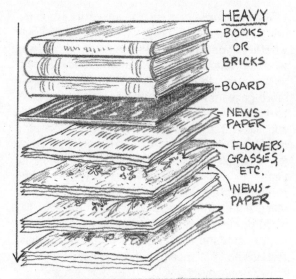

HEAVY
BOOKS
OR
BRICKS

BOARD

NEWS-
PAPER

FLOWERS,
GRASSES,
ETC.

NEWS-
PAPER

Do you like flowers and shells and seedpods and all sorts of little lacy leaves and grasses? You can have a good time collecting them, preserving them, and turning them into beautiful and useful things. Use Mother Nature's bounty to make greeting cards, place cards, bookmarks, and note paper.

You Will Need
    paper and cardboard
    white glue
    clear adhesive film (like Con-tac)
    facial tissue
    razor or x-acto knife
    metal ruler
    clear lacquer spray

To start, you will have to gather your natural materials. You may already have some things that you can use. If you're like me, you can't resist picking up little seashells and have stashes of them around the house. Start gathering small flowers. Delicate, lacy ones are best, though there are some large flowers, too, that can be used. Plants like hydrangeas, which can be separated into individual blossom heads, are useful. Gather a variety of leaves, grasses, and ferns. Again, look for interesting shapes. Don't pass up weeds; they are often very beautiful.

JULY
ONE WEEK

To dry and press your harvest, you will need a lot of newspaper and some heavy books or some bricks. Cut the newspaper into sheets about the same size as the books. Place some flowers on several layers of newspaper. If a flower has a heavy center, see if you can cut some of the thickness away on the back without destroying its shape or making the flower fall apart. Flowers with many layers of petals are not good for drying whole, but you can pull them apart and dry the petals separately. Then they can be reassembled when you glue them to the card. Don't crowd the flowers on the newspaper. Cover them with about four layers of newspaper and lay out some more leaves and flowers. Continue to add layers of newspaper and leaves and flowers until they are all taken care of. Top the pile with a piece of board and weight it down with bricks or a stack of heavy books. Leave them between the layers of newspaper for about a week, or until they are pressed flat and completely dry. Some plants take longer to dry than others. Some flowers fade as they dry; others stay beautiful and bright. You will soon learn which ones dry the best.

24

Greeting Cards

If it is not already folded, fold a small piece of note paper so that it fits into its envelope. Arrange dried flowers and leaves in a pleasing design on the cover of the folded card. If you wish to write something on the cover, do it now. Use indelible ink or a waterproof felt pen. Fix the flowers and leaves in place with dabs of white glue. In a small pan, dilute some white glue with water. Use about one part glue to two parts water. Insert a piece of waxed paper in the fold, between the front and back of the card. Now separate the two layers of a facial tissue and lay one over your card. Gently brush on the diluted glue, starting from the center and working out until the entire front of the card is covered. The glue will soak through the tissue and adhere it to the card. Leave as few air bubbles as possible. The tissue will wrinkle, but that is okay; it's part of the effect. Set the card in a warm place until it is dry. Trim away the excess tissue and press the card, just the way you did the flowers, until it is nice and flat. These cards look best if your designs are very simple. Use flowers and leaves with distinct outlines and ones that are in strong contrast to the background.

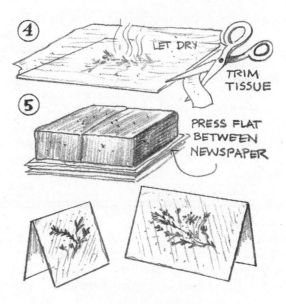

Bookmarks

Cut a strip of colored construction paper the right size for a bookmark, about 2 inches by 7 inches. Arrange some dried flowers, grasses, or leaves on it in a pleasing design. Hold them in place with small dabs of glue. Cut a piece of transparent self-adhesive film the same length as the bookmark but twice as wide. Lift one side of the film away from its backing and carefully position your bookmark between the film and the backing so that all the edges line up exactly. Smooth the film over the bookmark. Now remove the rest of the backing and fold the film over to cover the back of the bookmark. Use only plant material that will press very flat for these so that there are no ugly air pockets left under the film.

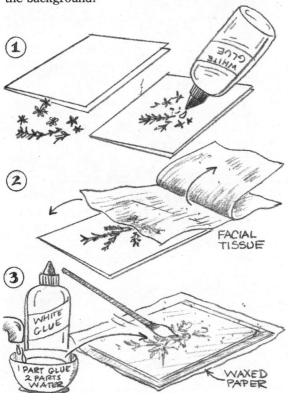

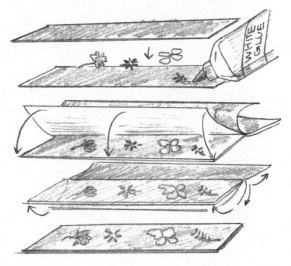

Place Cards

Place cards are the easiest to make because the decorations don't have to be flat. This is a good way to use pretty little seashells or seedpods. Use some fairly heavy white cardboard and cut it into pieces about 2 inches by 5 inches. Measure and make light pencil marks 1 inch in on either side. Hold a ruler along the pencil lines and gently score (cut into part way) the cardboard with a razor knife. Bend the cardboard along the score line, so that it stands up. Decorate the left side of the place card with tiny shells, seedpods, or a small dried flower. Glue them on well with white glue. Leave plenty of space to write names. Since place cards are used only once, you don't need to cover the dried flowers with film or tissue, but you might spray them with several coats of clear lacquer to make them slightly more durable.

Package the greeting cards and envelopes separately in plastic wrap. Note paper should be wrapped six to a package. Have a nice selection of different flowers in each pack. Bookmarks can be sold separately and will need no packaging. Wrap up a batch of twelve place cards as shown. Gift cards can be sold separately or in packages of three or six. Take samples to stationery stores and gift shops and ask the owners if they will sell them for you. Work out the prices so that you both will make some money on them.

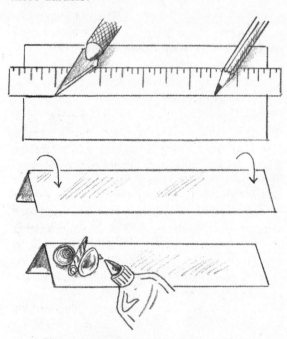

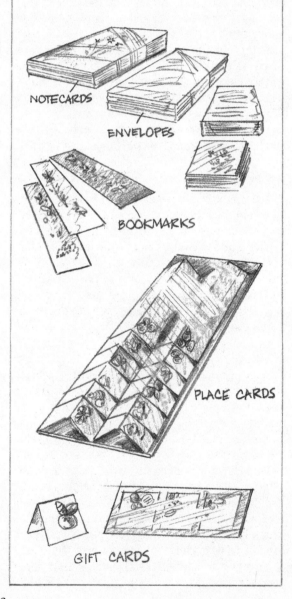

NOTECARDS

ENVELOPES

BOOKMARKS

PLACE CARDS

GIFT CARDS

SINCE GIFT CARDS DON'T HAVE TO FIT INTO ENVELOPES OR BE MAILED, YOU CAN MAKE THESE CARDS THE WAY YOU DID THE PLACE CARDS.

The Dawn Patrol School Escort Service

Are you one of those early-bird types who gets up bright and shiny and all set to start the day? (Slugabeds need not read this.) If you are, you might go into business taking little kids to school. Lots of parents who work have to leave home before it's time for their children to start for school. You could take a big worry off their minds and earn some money at the same time. Offer to walk their little ones to school every day.

How to Get Started

First of all, find out where the grade schools and nursery schools are in your neighborhood and what time they open. If there is one nearby and the timing doesn't conflict with your own school hours, you may be in business. Talk to several of the teachers. Tell them what you have in mind and ask them to tell parents who might be interested in your service. Ask if you can put up a notice on the school bulletin board. If you make a good impression and have some character references from people whose kids you babysit, the teacher will probably be happy to help you. Go to neighbors who have little kids and tell them about your service.

Your biggest problem will be setting up a schedule that works for everybody. Some parents may have to leave very early, long before time for school. In those cases, you may find it works best to have them drop their children off at your house. Other kids can be picked up as you go. You will have to figure out how long it takes you to get from one place to the next. Don't forget when you are estimating time that little kids don't walk as fast as you do. You'll have to allow some time for picking up leaves, inspecting bugs, and wading in puddles.

The number of kids you can take depends on how well organized you are. Start by thinking about all the things that might go wrong, then think about ways to prevent them.

Problem: The child is never ready when you get there and makes everyone else late for school. (This is one you are sure to run into.) Solution: Tell the parents before you start that you will not wait for any child more than once.

Problem: How do you deal with a child who persistently does not obey, runs away from the group, or hits other children. Solution: Tell the parents that you can no longer take the child because you cannot control his or her behavior. Tell them that you don't feel comfortable with the situation since you are responsible for all the children's safety. Word it so it doesn't sound like you are blaming the child or them.

Problem: How do you keep the group together, moving in the right direction. Solution: Establish rules right from the beginning. Use the "buddy" system: divide the kids up into pairs who hold each other's hands and who are responsible for each other. Pair calm children with wild ones. Have them walk in a line with the most responsible pair bringing up the rear. Make the walk fun. Have the kids pretend they are elephants or ducklings or a marching band.

Problem: You have a large, busy street to cross. Solution: Talk to the kids ahead of time about how they are to cross the street and about safety. Talk about how they are never to run and how they are always to cross with the light. Have a special street-crossing formation, with responsible kids at the head and end of the line. You walk across in the middle, where you can watch both ends.

Schedule		3/1/90 - 3/31/90
Name	Address	Time
Joan	my house	7:15 M-F
Teddy	my house	7:30 Tu-Th-F
Patrick	10 Lower Lane	8:30 M-F
Alice	16 Lower Lane	8:35 M-F
Sandy	106 Prospect	8:38 M-F
Carl	117 Prospect	8:40 M-Tu-Th
Mattie	65 State St.	8:42 M-F
John	62 State St.	not coming until 4/2/90
Amelia	59 State St.	8:45 M-S

Problem: You arrive at the school and there is no one there to take care of the children. Solution: *Stay with the children until someone arrives. Never leave little kids unattended.* You can always explain or get a note to explain why you are late.

If you build up your business until it's too much to handle alone, get a friend to come in with you. This will provide a front and rear guard and make everything easier, safer, and more fun.

You could make your Dawn Patrol group more visible and safer at street crossings by having a uniform. Make up a bunch of bright red or orange bibs like the ones highway workers wear. The kids will love them, and it will be good advertising for your business.

What to Charge

Charge a weekly fee for the school escort service based on how many days a week you take the child. Some nursery school children may go only two or three times a week. If children are left at your home for any length of time in the morning, you should add your regular babysitting charge to the escort fee. Start with only a few kids, until you see if you are going to be able to handle the job and still get to school on time yourself.

The High-Times Kite Company

There are some days when everybody should go fly a kite. Not the mean kind of "Oh, go fly a kite!" days, but the good kind. That's when a proper kite company should have a big supply of all sorts of kites on hand. If you decide to go into the kite business, start to make up your stock right away because you never know when that great kite day will come along. Make a variety of sizes and designs and colors. Then when the sky is blue and the wind is just right, go out there and sell them.

You probably already know how to make many kinds of kites, so I won't give you instructions but will just tell you about some of the things I've seen kids do to make them a little different. If you aren't an experienced kite-maker, there are lots of books on the subject in the library. Make up some samples to test-fly, and then use your most successful designs as models for the ones you plan to sell.

Minikites, tiny versions of full-size kites, are fun to make. Little kids especially love them because they'll fly on very short lengths of string. They'll practically fly indoors. You can use soda straws or shaved-down strips of bamboo, anything that is very narrow and lightweight, for the sticks. String them with heavy-duty sewing thread and cover them with clear plastic wrap or with tissue paper. Tails can be made with thread and tissue paper or with thin Mylar ribbon.

You can make regular-size kites out of plain white paper (rice paper is strong and comes in large sheets) and decorate them by gluing on patches of bright-colored tissue paper. Leave a rectangle of white paper, where the owner's name can be written with a felt pen. Make your decorations big and bold so you can still see them when the kite is in the air.

If you're a pretty good artist, make portrait kites. Have a supply of plain white kites. When you sell one, use felt pens to draw a face that looks like the new owner. Make big funny faces with smiling mouths. They don't really have to look like the person, but give them the right color hair and eyes. Look for something special about each person, such as glasses or freckles or a hat, that you can put in your portrait.

Save Mylar wrapping paper at Christmastime or buy some Mylar sheets at the art store. It makes wonderful glittery kites. You can use Mylar ribbons for tails.

Try some of the bird-shaped kites. They are fairly easy to make and are good flyers. The ones shown in kite books are often covered with fabric, but they can be made of paper just as well. Cover them with plain white paper and then glue on black-and-white tissue-paper feathers to make them look like hawks or seagulls.

How to Sell Your Kites

If you have a special kite hill in your town or a playground where people congregate, load your kites in a wagon and go out there on the first windy day. Have one of your best kites flying if there's a steady wind and you don't have to attend to it all the time. If the wind is variable, tending your kite will take too much of your time, and you won't be able to concentrate on selling. Make a sign and attach it to a stick, or fasten it to the wagon so it won't blow away. Have all of your kites clearly marked with prices.

KITES   KITES   KITES
BIG KITES   MIDDLE-SIZE KITES
MINIKITES
COME AND GET 'EM WHILE THEY LAST!
25¢ TO $5.00

What you charge will depend on the size and how well made your kites are. Minikites should sell for no more than a quarter. Large Mylar or bird kites, if they are strongly made and are good flyers, could be sold for $4.00 to $5.00. Sell balls of string for 10¢ to 20¢ more than you paid for them and lengths of well-sanded, 1-inch doweling for rolling the string on for 10¢ each.

WEEKENDERS

The Best Babysitters Ever!

This is a way you can turn an old idea into a brand-new business and make work that might be boring into something enjoyable for everyone. Most kids do babysitting at one time or another. Well, if you can do babysitting, you can certainly start a Weekend Babysitters Co-op. What's that? That's where you and a friend invite mothers or dads you know to leave their children at your house during the day on Saturday or Sunday while they go shopping or to the football game or just have a day to themselves. Instead of just sitting, you organize games and projects for the kids and have a fine old time. Here's how.

First, get together with a friend and plan how your co-op will work. You'll need to decide when you want to do it, whose house it will be in, what activities to plan for the kids, and who to tell about it.

Let people know about your service at least a week in advance. Start by calling your regular customers or by going to see them. You could also put notices at their doors. Have people call you ahead of time so you'll know how many kids to plan for. Don't take on more kids than you can handle comfortably. Or have another person lined up who will come to help out if you get too big a crowd for you alone.

BABYSITTING SPECIAL!
SATURDAY, NOVEMBER 18
12 - 5 PM

GOING TO THE GAME? BRING YOUR KIDS TO OUR CO-OP FIRST. CALL FRANK HILL - 956-1235 OR JENNY BANKS - 954-3211 ▶ BY WEDNESDAY, NOVEMBER 15 ◀ TO SAVE A SPOT FOR YOUR CHILD. $2.00/HR.

Let's have a puppet show!

Yeah! We could bake cookies too.

On the big day have one room set up for your co-op, like a family room or basement playroom. If it's winter, have a place for the kids to put their coats and boots. In the summer you will want to go outdoors, so have your co-op in a place where there is a fenced yard or somewhere protected from the street.

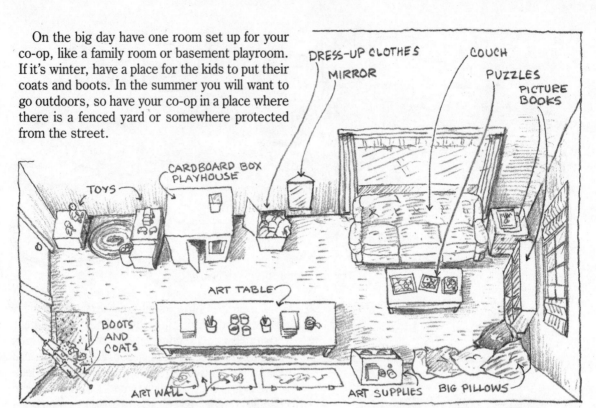

DRESS-UP CLOTHES
MIRROR
COUCH
PUZZLES
PICTURE BOOKS
TOYS
CARDBOARD BOX PLAYHOUSE
BOOTS AND COATS
ART TABLE
ART WALL
ART SUPPLIES
BIG PILLOWS

Indoor Activities

Remember to plan ahead so you'll have the supplies you need. Use stuff you have around the house—old crayons and chalk, newspapers and paper bags—and keep what you buy to a minimum so you don't spend more than you make. You can often scrounge supplies if you go to the right places. Newspapers will often give you the leftovers from their big rolls of paper. Printing companies are another good place to ask for paper. They often have stacks of paper that has been trimmed from larger sheets. Sometimes these scraps are pretty colors. They are usually happy to give it away to anyone who has a good use for it.

Help kids make gifts for their parents: cards, pictures, tin-can pencil holders.

Paint a group portrait. Do it on newsprint or paper bags that have been taped together and then taped to the wall. Or at paint-supply stores you can buy paper drop cloths like the ones painters use. If you use paints, have a bunch of old shirts for smocks.

Have extra things around for kids to play with if they don't want to be part of the group: crayons and paper, books, toys, puzzles.

A playhouse is usually a favorite with little kids. You can make a nifty one out of the cardboard cartons that appliances like stoves and dishwashers come packed in.

You Will Need
   a large cardboard carton
   a sharp razor knife
   brown paper packing tape
   paint and brushes
   two spools
   string

First, cut the door and windows and a square hole in the roof for a chimney. Bend the door in both directions so that it will open and close easily. Do the same with the shutters on the windows. Fasten spool doorknobs with string to both sides of the door. Cut a letter slot in the center so the kids can drop letters through it.

Make a chimney out of a small box with the top and bottom cut out and tape it securely in place. Make it sturdy because part of the fun is dropping things down the chimney.

Now, paint the house. You could paint flowered wallpaper inside and pictures on the walls. The outside could be brick or stone, with the shutters and door a bright color. You will be surprised how much fun the children will have with this and how much fun you'll have making it.

Have a talent show or a costume parade or a skit. Collect some old clothes and hats for dressing up. You might organize a play to give for the parents at the end of the day. If you do plan a play, tell the parents ahead of time so they can plan to stay a little while when they come to pick up their children.

Make cookies. This is a big project that can easily go wrong unless you plan it very carefully. Pick out a simple sugar-cookie recipe that you have tried before. Make sure you have all the ingredients and lots of space for the kids to work. Let the kids help with stirring and shaping and decorating the cookies. Decorate them with food coloring (a few drops added to the batter), raisins, nuts, chocolate chips, or jam.

Outdoor Activities

Outdoor babysitting is easier in some ways and harder in others. Outside you don't have to worry about the mess, but it's often harder to ensure that nothing goes wrong. Plan your outdoor activities just as carefully as you do your indoor ones.

Building sand castles is good outdoor fun. You'll need a pile or a box of fine sand. Make sure that it is clean by sifting it through an old screen to get the pebbles and junk out. Always leave it covered with a tarp when it's not in use so the kitties don't get into it. The evening or morning before your castle building, sprinkle the sand with the hose until it's just damp enough to hold together. Find a bunch of plastic boxes, cups, and bowls of different shapes to use for molds. Some of the rubbery spatulas you use to scrape mixing bowls are good tools for shaping sand. The children may want to work on their own castles, or they may want to build one large castle. Younger kids may want to make cakes and pies.

SOAP BUBBLES ARE ALWAYS POPULAR. YOU CAN MAKE GOOD BUBBLES WITH A LIQUID DETERGENT MIXED WITH WATER. COMBINE 2/3 CUPS DAWN LIQUID DETERGENT, 3 TEASPOONS GLYCERIN AND I GALLON WATER. LET IT STAND OVERNIGHT.

MAKE THE BUBBLE RINGS OUT OF TWISTED WIRE. HEAVIER GAUGE WIRE WORKS BETTER THAN THIN WIRE BECAUSE IT HOLDS MORE SOAP.

IF YOU HAVE A SMOOTH CEMENT SIDEWALK OR DRIVEWAY, IT CAN BE A GREAT CANVAS FOR CHALK ART. HAVE THE KIDS LIE DOWN ON THE CEMENT WITH THEIR ARMS AND LEGS OUT IN FUNNY POSITIONS, TRACE THEIR OUTLINES AND LET THEM DRAW IN THEIR CLOTHES AND FACES WITH COLORED CHALK.

BIG THICK PIECES OF CHALK ARE THE BEST ON CEMENT.

You probably won't always end up with a group of kids the same age, so you may have to plan different activities for different kids. One of you might have to handle the younger kids and the other the older ones. If people bring babies or crawlers, you'll need someone to take care of them—maybe you could take turns or, if lots of kids are coming, get a third friend to help. Get a playpen to keep crawlers out of trouble.

Plan a quiet time for all of the kids and for you. (Maybe you could have a special quiet room for babies' naps.) Try to plan 15 or 20 minutes when everyone lies down to rest or does quiet things such as look at picture books or listen to music. Or you could gather everyone around you and read them a story.

Some Safety Precautions

1. *Definitely* have the emergency numbers for the police, fire department, ambulance, and poison control center. The numbers should be posted near the telephone.

2. If possible, have an emergency telephone number of someone to call for each child.

3. Find an adult in the neighborhood who will agree to be available to help in case of an emergency.

4. Have a first aid kit around to take care of small accidents.

5. *Never* leave children unattended, no matter how safe it seems.

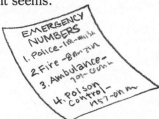

Discipline Problems

Never spank or hit children in your care, no matter how naughty they are. You are smarter and bigger and should be able to think of a better way to handle any situation.

A "cooling-off" place, where kids can go if they are messing up and getting into trouble, usually works very well. It should be where you can keep an eye on the child but private enough so he or she will feel removed from the action. Have some pillows to sit on and books to look at. Let the child stay there until he or she has calmed down and is ready to rejoin the group. It shouldn't take long, especially if the other children are doing something that looks like fun.

Sometimes a little humor will change a child's mood and avoid a tantrum. Keep a box of raisins in your pocket, and if trouble threatens, give the child a raisin and tell him that it's a "happy pill."

If, in spite of all you can do, a child is rough and disruptive and upsets the other children, you will just have to manage as well as you can until the parents come. However, the next time the parents ask you to sit for their child, you certainly don't have to. Tell them politely that you don't seem to be able to control the child and cannot take that responsibility.

HERE ARE SOME THINGS TO THINK ABOUT.

1. Try to have more than enough activities planned. After you've done the Weekend Co-op a few times, you'll have a better idea of how long activities will take to do.

2. Start out slowly until you get an idea of how many children you can comfortably handle.

3. When you've had a couple of co-op days for people you already know, you may want to expand your business. You could put little flyers on the bulletin boards in grocery stores and laundromats advertising your service.

4. Be sure to keep track of how long each kid stays so you'll know how much to charge the parents.

The Stuff and Junk Company

What can you do with bottle caps? Or tin cans? What kind of nifty things can you make out of old newspapers? How could you make an old T-shirt, torn bed sheet, or holey bath towel into something useful? Some of the best ideas for things to do (and ways to make money) come from the junk heap. If you think about it for a while, you'll come up with your own ideas. But while you're thinking, here are some ideas we know about that you could try. Once you get going, you can make a good after-school or Saturday business out of making miracles out of junk and other stuff, and selling them in your neighborhood.

Toy Boats for Toddlers

Here is a project using scrap wood that you can scrounge from a building site or from the discard bin at your local lumberyard. By the way, it's always smart to ask someone if you can take things, even though they are obviously scrap. This fleet of toy boats can be made from pieces of lumber too small to be of any other use.

Since these boats are designed to be used on the floor and not in the water, you don't have to worry about making them seaworthy. The hulls are made of flat boards; two-by-fours are a good size. The prows are cut into a point and sanded well to make them smooth. You can build tankers by adding a small superstructure at the stern, or passenger ships by adding several layers of cabin decks. Dowels or small square trim pieces make good smokestacks. Sand all the pieces well before you assemble them; it's much easier than trying to sand afterward. Put the boats together with nails and a good wood glue. Nails alone will work loose with rough play. Paint your boats with bright colors, and add some embellishments. Big, round upholstery tacks make excellent portholes.

You will have to decide how much to charge for your boats, based on how long it takes you to make them and how well they are made. If you take a lot of time and trouble sanding all the pieces, put them together solidly, and paint them very carefully, you can charge a lot more than if they are made quickly and will break soon.

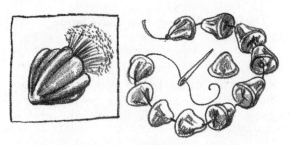

Eucalyptus-Pod Flea Collars

If you live where eucalyptus trees grow, you can make organic flea collars for dogs and cats. Fleas don't like the smell of eucalyptus pods. Dogs and people don't mind it at all. So instead of putting collars full of poison around their animals' necks, your customers could use collars that smell nice and that won't hurt anyone but the fleas.

Use pods that are green with fuzzy beards. The smell of those lasts longest, but even pods that have turned dark and gotten hard will work. Punch holes through the pods from front to back with an ice pick or awl. String the pods on a length of fine elastic. You may want to make several sizes. You can make the collars with string and just tie them around the animal's neck with a bowknot, but the elastic is safer as it allows the animal to pull free if the collar gets caught on something. Sell the collars for $2.00 each.

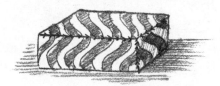

Dumpster Doorstops

Almost every house has a door that bangs shut when the wind blows. It's not only noisy, but it's often inconvenient, and if the family cat happens to be going in or out at the time, it could be the beginning of a woeful tail. You can make useful and decorative doorstops out of old bricks.

First, the brick should be padded with some sort of scrap material. Sew it neatly around the brick. Then cover the brick with a piece of pretty decorative fabric. You may want to start with very simple doorstops that are covered only with fabric. Later, you might want to make fancier ones and experiment with braid borders, appliqué, embroidery, or needlepoint.

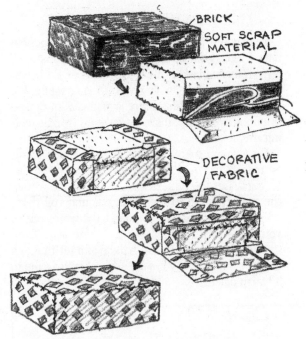

Bottle-Cap Door Mat

If you can collect enough of them, bottle caps make a good doormat. The best place to get caps is wherever there is a soft-drink machine. Any kind of cap works, even the twist-off kind.

Get a board about 16 by 20 inches. Exterior-type plywood is the best, the kind that withstands water. It should be at least ⅝ inch thick. Drive a nail through the middle of each cap, nailing them to the board in rows, with the caps just touching one another. After all the caps are nailed in place, finish the mat with brown, black, or green spray paint. This kind of mat is perfect for scraping the mud off dirty boots or shoes. Sell each mat for $4.00 or more.

Newspaper Logs

Everyone has old newspapers. Many people have fireplaces, and firewood is very expensive to buy. You can make fireplace logs out of old newspapers that will burn almost as long as a pine log the same size. Unless there is an awful lot of free firewood around, you should have no trouble selling them.

Soak some folded newspapers (a stack about an inch thick) in a tub containing water and detergent. Let the papers soak until they're wet all the way through. Take them out and roll them around a broom handle. Squeeze the water out as you roll. Add a second layer the same way. Then gently remove the broom handle and let the logs dry thoroughly. (It will take several days, even in a warm place.)

The broomstick helps you make the log by giving you something to roll the paper around, but it also does something else that is important. When the log burns, the hole helps the heat reach the center of the log and burn it all the way through. The detergent is used to make the paper sticky enough so that it remains in the shape of a log, even after it dries.

First, make some samples and try them in your own fireplace, or get a neighbor to try them. See how long they burn. Make some bigger and some smaller, and see which one works best.

How much should you charge for your logs? That depends partly on you and partly on your customers. Make the price as low as you can. People will probably pay 50¢ per log, maybe more if they can't get firewood at a reasonable price.

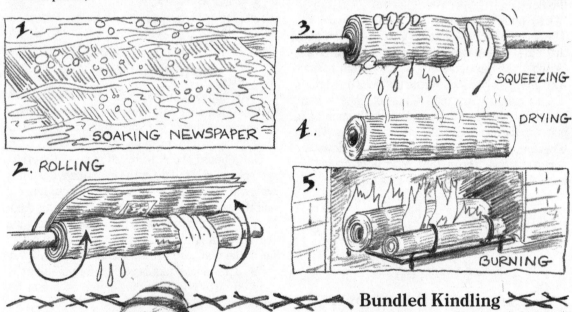

1. SOAKING NEWSPAPER

2. ROLLING

3. SQUEEZING

4. DRYING

5. BURNING

Bundled Kindling

This could be another moneymaker to go with your newspaper-log business. If you live near woods where you can find a lot of dry branches that have fallen off the trees, gather them. They make excellent kindling. Cut or break them into regular lengths and tie them up into uniform-size bundles. Old wooden shingles make even better kindling. Look for houses that are being remodeled where the roofs are being replaced. The carpenters will probably be glad to let you have as many of the old shingles as you can carry away. They are already cut into uniform lengths. All you have to do is break them into narrow sticks and tie them into bundles.

Helping Hands for the Happy Hostess

A party should be a happy occasion, but often the people who give one find that they're too tired or too busy to enjoy it. This is where you come in. Be a party helper. Offer to help with preparations, polishing silver, setting tables, making hors d'oeuvres, whatever needs doing. While the party is in progress, you could see that the serving platters are replenished, keep an eye on anything that's cooking, make coffee, pass food, and generally keep things tidy. Stick around to help with the postparty cleanup, or arrange to come back in the morning to help out.

Here are some things to think about.

1. Talk to your customer before the party. Find out what he or she wants you to do and approximately how long you will be needed. Tell your customer how much you charge per hour. Write down all of the particulars so you don't forget or get confused about times or dates.

2. On the day of the party, be there exactly when you said you would be.

3. Come dressed to work. If you are going to serve at the party, you might want to bring something fresh to change into just before the guests arrive. You should look neat and clean and not too dressed up.

4. Don't forget that you are there to work. Be friendly and polite, but don't hang around with the guests. Keep busy with your party chores.

5. When you are finished, check the time and write it down next to your arrival time. Figure out the number of hours that you have worked and multiply it by your hourly charge. Write out a bill showing your calculations and give it to your customer.

The best way to get into the party-help business is by offering your services to friends and neighbors, people who already know you. If you are reliable and do a good job, you will find that the people who come to their parties will ask for your name and start calling you in to help.

After you've been in business for a while and have a group of happy customers, you might start selling hors d'oeuvres as a sideline. Search through some cookbooks or ask your mom to show you some of her favorite recipes. Look for foods that can be prepared ahead of time, ones that will keep and not taste stale. Some things can be made ahead and frozen; then they can be defrosted and cooked the day of the party. Experiment with several kinds and figure out how long they take to prepare. Keep track of how much your ingredients cost and how many pieces the recipe makes. Decide how much you want to charge per hour for your labor, then add your labor cost to the price of your ingredients and figure out what to charge for each kind of hors d'oeuvre. Here are a couple of good recipes.

DRAGON WINGS

- 5 lbs. whole chicken wings
- 2 cups soy sauce
- 2 cups vegetable oil
- 3 tsp. sesame oil
- 1 tsp. black pepper
- 1 tblsp. sugar
- 4 tblsp. dry sherry
- 3 cloves garlic, minced
- 4 tblsp. grated fresh ginger (or 2 tsp. ground ginger.)

1. MIX ALL INGREDIENTS, EXCEPT THE CHICKEN, IN A LARGE BOWL.

If you can get fresh ginger, be sure to use it — the flavor is much nicer than the ground ginger that you find on the spice shelf.

2. DISJOINT THE CHICKEN WINGS AND DISCARD THE TIPS.

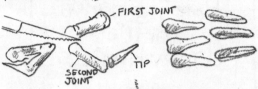

FIRST JOINT
SECOND JOINT
TIP

3. MARINATE THE FIRST AND SECOND JOINTS IN THE SOY MIXTURE FOR FOUR OR FIVE HOURS IN THE REFRIGERATOR, STIRRING OCCASIONALLY.

4 HOURS

4. DRAIN THEM AND PLACE THEM IN ONE LAYER IN SHALLOW BAKING PANS. THE PIECES SHOULD NOT TOUCH EACH OTHER.

5. BAKE AT 350 DEGREES FOR ABOUT AN HOUR, OR UNTIL THEY ARE NICELY BROWNED.

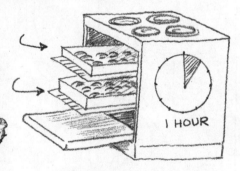

1 HOUR

6. DRAGON WINGS CAN BE SERVED WARM OR COLD. THEY'RE VERY GOOD AT ANY TEMPERATURE.

PUT ALL OF THE LITTLE DRUMSTICK-LIKE FIRST JOINTS ON ONE PLATTER AND THE SECOND JOINTS ON ANOTHER. (THEY LOOK BETTER THAT WAY.)
DECORATE THE PLATTERS WITH FRESH PARSLEY.

CHEESE CRISPIES

- 1 lb. sharp Cheddar cheese, at room temperature
- ¼ lb. butter, soft
- 2 tsp. Worcestershire sauce
- ¼ tsp. Tabasco sauce, or other pepper sauce
- ¾ tsp. salt
- 1½ cups flour

1. GRATE THE CHEESE AND CREAM IT WITH THE BUTTER.

2. ADD THE WORCESTERSHIRE SAUCE, TABASCO SAUCE AND SALT. CREAM UNTIL SMOOTH AND THOROUGHLY BLENDED.

3. ADD THE FLOUR AND MIX UNTIL THE DOUGH HOLDS TOGETHER.

4. REFRIGERATE COVERED FOR SEVERAL HOURS, OR EVEN FOR SEVERAL DAYS.

5. WHEN YOU ARE READY TO BAKE THE CRISPIES, ROLL THE DOUGH INTO SMALL BALLS, ABOUT THE SIZE OF MARBLES.

THIS RECIPE SHOULD MAKE ABOUT 75 TO 100.

6. PUT THE MARBLES OF DOUGH ON A COOKIE SHEET AND PRESS EACH ONE WITH THE TINES OF A FORK UNTIL IT IS A LITTLE STRIPED WAFER ABOUT THE SIZE OF A QUARTER.

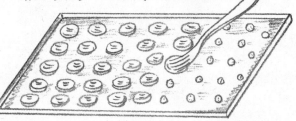

7. BAKE AT 475 DEGREES FOR EIGHT TO TEN MINUTES.

THE CHEESE CRISPIES CAN BE SERVED WARM, OR THEY CAN BE BAKED SEVERAL DAYS IN ADVANCE AND STORED IN A TIN.

The library is a good place to look for more hors d'oeuvre recipes. There are several new books that are full of suggestions for interesting foods to make for parties and exciting ways to serve them.

The Backward Papergirl

Jacqueline White has a paper route in reverse. She lives in Milwaukee, Wisconsin, and believes that people need trees just as much as they need newspapers. She has arranged to collect papers from people in her neighborhood on a regular schedule; then she takes them to a collection center which ships them back to a mill where they are made into more newsprint. It's a pretty good idea, and it's one of the ways Jacqueline earns money. Just like a paper route—only backward. Of course, this will work only if there isn't already a free recycling pickup in your area.

First, look in the yellow pages in your telephone book under "Waste Paper" and find the nearest recycling company. Ask how much the company pays for newspapers. It will probably be about $25.00 per 500 pounds. That sounds like a lot of newspapers, but paper is heavy, and it should be fairly easy to collect that much in a very

short while. Some companies will pay for magazines and corrugated cardboard as well.

Make up a little advertisement to take around to all the houses in your neighborhood. Say something like this:

> **PLEASE HELP ME SAVE TREES I HAVE A BACKWARD PAPER ROUTE. ONCE EVERY TWO WEEKS I WILL COLLECT ALL YOUR OLD PAPERS AND TAKE THEM TO A PLACE THAT MAKES THEM INTO NEW PAPER. CALL SANDRA IF YOU WANT THIS SERVICE. MY PHONE IS: 446-1085**

Figure out how many newspapers you want in a bundle. Keep it to a size that you can lift easily. Be sure to use good strong twine (not string) for your bundles so they won't come apart. Collect the bundles in a wagon and stack them in your garage, or wherever there is room out of the rain. If you make all the bundles the same size, you can very easily figure out how many pounds you have. Weigh one bundle on your bathroom scale and multiply that weight by the number of bundles you have collected. When you have about 500 pounds, ask a grown-up friend to help you take them to the collection center.

The White-Tornado Basement Cleaners and Garage Sale Company

Here are two ideas in one. First, cleaning basements or garages and hauling away the junk. Second, selling the junk you haul away from the places you clean. Try it as a weekend business. Clean basements on Saturdays until you have gathered enough good junk to sell. Then have a giant garage sale the next Saturday. You can make money both ways.

Idea Number 1: Cleaning Basements and Garages

First, make a list of everyone you and your friends can think of who has a basement or garage or attic that might need a good cleaning. Then make signs or notices that tell about your business. Put them where people will see them. When someone calls you up, be sure to tell that person how many workers you will bring, what cleaning materials you can bring, and what tools or materials your customer may have to provide.

Here is an "attack" plan for the big cleanup.

1. Arrive on time ready to work. Tell the customer how much you will charge for the job after you have looked it over and discussed what needs to be done. If you have already made an estimate, remind the customer what you agreed to. Charge about $10.00 for a small job and $15.00 for a large one. (Practice on your own basement first so you'll know how long the job takes.)

2. Ask your customer to show you which things are to be kept and which are to be taken away when you clean. Be sure to ask if it's okay to keep some of the take-aways for your sale. (If your customers know that you have a use for them, they may decide to let you take away more things.)

3. Sort out the room. Put the take-aways into boxes for hauling away and the trash into trash containers. Stack the things to be kept by the customer neatly in one corner.

4. Dust and sweep the room

5. Scrub any shelves, doors, and windows

43

with a solution of trisodium phosphate and water. Rinse them with clear water. Wear rubber gloves, or you'll end up with sore hands.

6. Mop the floor with the same solution. If there is grease on the floor, you may have to use a stronger solution and hot water. Don't use solvents such as paint thinner. The fumes are bad for you, and the risk of fire is too great.

7. Ask your customer to check your work before he or she pays you. Be sure to haul away the discards and trash immediately. That's part of the job.

When you have collected lots of take-aways, you should start to think about:

Idea Number 2: The Great Garage Sale

Be sure to have your sale on a weekend, either Saturday or Saturday and Sunday. Don't choose a holiday weekend. (Too many people go away.) The day before the sale, put up posters around your neighborhood. (Be sure to take them down again when your sale is over.) Use the bulletin boards in laundromats and grocery stores and the library. Put up notices at school and church. Make a big banner or sign to put out in front on the day of the sale.

Choose a place that is as close as possible to the sidewalk, where it can be seen from the street. If it won't bother the neighbors, play music on the radio to make the sale cheery. You might offer coffee or lemonade to the people who come. The idea is to make your customers as comfortable and welcome as you can.

Things to sell. You need to know that there are two kinds of junk. *Good junk* is what one person asks you to haul away, but another person will pay 10¢ for. *Junk junk* is what no one wants. Sometimes it's a little hard to know the difference, but it's important to learn the difference if you are going to have a really good garage sale. Here are some examples.

One wire hanger is *junk junk*. Twelve wire hangers neatly stacked and tied with twisties or

44

string is *good junk*. Charge 20 cents. Twelve wooden hangers neatly stacked and tied is *very good junk*. Charge $2.00.

Loose items like wood screws and other fasteners aren't worth much, but if you collect a jar of wood screws, you can sell it for 25¢ to 30¢. The same is true for baby-food jars, *National Geographics*, and lots of other things. They are worth more in bunches.

Magazines will sell best if they are sorted by title and year and sold as sets. Look for old copies of *Life*, *Look*, *Saturday Evening Post*, or *Colliers*. Any of the glossy, pretty magazines like *Architectural Digest* or *Town and Country* also sell well.

Look for clay flowerpots. New flowerpots are expensive, so used ones are very, very good junk. Scrub them inside and out and sell them at half the new price. Plastic and metal ones are not so good, but you might be able to sell some in sets of six-of-a-kind.

Small furniture items, even if they need some repair, are a good bet. People will buy things like wooden chairs (the kitchen kind), small tables, and dressers to fix up. Clean them up as best you can before the sale.

Clothespins packaged twelve to a baggie and tied with yarn will sell for 15¢ to 20¢ per bag. Old wooden ones can be made to look like new if you soak them in water with some bleach added and then let them dry in the sun.

Kitchen tools should be washed and the metal parts scoured to make them bright. Things that come in sets, like knives and spoons and forks or measuring cups, should be tied together and priced as one item.

Arrange your items in groups on tables or on the floor. Put things that are alike near one another. Be sure that everything is marked with a price or that your prices are clearly displayed on a poster.

The Kids' Flea Market

The chances are that when your friends see how successful you are with your garage sale, they'll want to join in the fun and have a huge Saturday Kids' Flea Market. If a lot of your friends want to sell things, you may have to move your market into the backyard. If so, big signs out front and a lot of word-of-mouth advertising will be very important.

Use the experience you gained from running your garage sale to help the other kids set up their booths. Tell your friends to bring their own card tables (or boxes with a board stretched across) to display their wares. Arrange the tables around the edges of the yard so the bargain hunters have lots of room. Encourage a friend to set up a refreshment stand. (Shoppers get hungry.) Since this is a Kids' Flea Market, you should sell the kinds of things that kids want to buy: old toys, outgrown clothes, books, jewelry, tricycles, posters, roller skates, dolls, pencils, pens, and so on. Tell your friends that it's a great way to clean out their rooms.

How do you make money running a flea market? One way is to charge each person who is selling things at your market a fee, like 50¢. Another way is to charge a percentage of what each person makes. If you charge your friends 10 percent of their profits, it's easy to figure out what they owe you. Say, for example, that someone makes $3.40, you just move the decimal point one place to the left and get 34¢. Someone who made $5.25 would owe you 53¢. If 10 percent seems like too much to take, you might charge only 5 percent. Then all you need to do is figure the 10 percent and divide it in half. Or you may decide that you won't charge them anything because the bigger the sale the more people come and the more everybody sells, including you. Oh yes! Make sure all of your friends agree to help you clean up the backyard when the flea market closes.

46

The City Dog Exercise Company

If you were a dog, your idea of heaven would probably be to be outdoors sniffing the air, the trees, the grass, or playing fetch, or having someone scratch your ears or your belly, or that place on your back just where your tail starts— that place you can't scratch by yourself. Well, gang, if you live in a city and like dogs, you can do your dog friends, your human neighbors, and yourself a favor by starting a really good dog-walking service.

Running a really good dog-walking service is very simple, but there are four important rules to follow. You must always be on time for your appointments, you must be polite to the human customers, you must be kind to the dog customers, and you must make sure that none of the dogs gets away from you or into trouble.

Advertise to get your first customers. Pick an apartment building or some other place where people have dogs and no yard. Try to find people who work all week and need their weekends to do other things. They are the ones who need your service the most.

Start small. You've probably seen professional dog walkers in big cities. They have lots of dogs on leashes. They stagger around, and no one has any fun. Dogs are smart animals. They know better. Treat each dog like the intelligent animal he or she is. Each is different. See what they like best, and try to make the walk the most fun you can. Never take more than two dogs at a time. At first, until you get to know the dogs, don't take more than one.

Find good dog places. Dogs get bored like anyone else, and nothing is as boring to a dog as being indoors all the time. So when you take dogs outside, take them to interesting dog places: places with grass, empty lots, the spaces behind buildings or under bridges, parks where there are people and children, playgrounds.

Know how to avoid trouble. Start by knowing what your dogs can and can't do. Most cities have passed ordinances that make it unlawful for dogs to use sidewalks as "bathrooms." Some cities don't want dogs in parks. Some have strict leash laws. Find out about these things by calling the local Humane Society or City Hall. Pay attention to these laws. Remember that each dog owner is trusting you with a member of the family. That's a responsibility. Never go off, even for a minute, and leave dogs alone, even if you tie them up.

Use short leashes. Bring along your own leash. The short kind is best because it is easier to hold and won't tangle. If you come to a place where it is permitted and you know the dog won't run away from you, you can let it run without having to take the leash off.

Give yourself a break. If you charge $1.50 for fifty minutes, that means you can take a ten-minute break each hour. You could do four dogs in a morning. That means $6.00. If you find that you can take two dogs at once, that's $12.00. Pretty good pay for half a Saturday's work! But give yourself that ten-minute break between dogs. You'll need it.

47

The Clearview Window Washers

This is an idea that will work if you live in a neighborhood with houses. If you live where there's nothing but twenty-story apartment buildings, you had better forget it. Since most grown-ups don't like to wash windows and many older people don't want to climb ladders, even the three-step kind, a window-washing business can be a great success. It's not hard work, and, especially if the windows are very dirty, it's actually sort of fun. It makes everything look so much brighter.

You Will Need
- **a ladder**
- **window cleaner or ammonia**
- **newspapers or nonlinty rags**
- **a sponge**
- **a squeegee**
- **a bucket**

You can buy spray bottles of commercial window cleaner, but it's cheaper to make your own with hot water and household ammonia. Put this mixture in a pump spray bottle; it works just as well as commercial cleaners. Spray the windows and then dry them with squares of newspaper or with rags. Ask your mom for some rags that don't leave a lot of lint (fuzz). If the windows are large, like sliding glass doors, or if they're very dirty, it's probably easier to mix up a bucketful of ammonia and hot water. Use a sponge to wash the windows and a squeegee to dry them. Finish off the corners and sides where the squeegee leaves drips with a rag.

Different people have different techniques with the squeegee. Some people go from top to bottom and some from side to side. You'll have to experiment to see which way works best for you.

A narrow squeegee is easier to handle, less tiring, and works for smaller windows as well.

Stepladders are expensive, so borrow one if you can. The folding aluminum ones, about 6 feet high with a shelf for your rags and cleaner, are the easiest to handle. They stand more solidly than short ladders, and you can reach most first-floor windows without climbing to the top rung. Don't agree to do the outside of second-story windows where you have to use an extension ladder or sit on the windowsill or climb out on a sloping roof.

One of the best things about this business is that it's very easy to see who needs you. Just look around. But be tactful. People don't like to be told that they have dirty windows, so just ask politely if they'd like to have their windows washed.

Tell your mother's friends (and your friends' mothers) about your business. Tell your neighbors. If you're acquainted with people who own stores in your neighborhood, tell them too.

Make a little notice with your name and phone number that you can give to people. Take it to real estate agents. Tell them you think people who come to look at houses for sale like to see clean windows. (That one works!)

You should keep your prices as reasonable as you can. That will encourage people to have you do their windows often. There are two ways to charge: by the window or by the hour. By the window, you could charge 50¢ for medium-size ones with only two panes and 60¢ to 75¢ if they have a lot of little panes. Charge more for very big windows and less for little ones. By the hour, charge $2.00 to $2.50, depending on how experienced you are. If you work very fast and don't leave streaks or spots, charge more. Charge a little less at first until you get good at it.

Special Hints

Don't agree to do the outside of second-story windows where you have to use an extension ladder, sit on the windowsill, or climb out on a sloping roof. It's too dangerous.

Never lean your ladder against the glass, only on the wall or on the frame. No one will ask you back if you break a window the first time.

Clean both sides of each window. If you have to go inside the house to do it, be very careful not to spill cleaner on the floors or carpets. Have a plastic drop cloth to put down under the window while you clean it.

Work quickly, but do a good job. Clean windows make everyone cheerful. Check your work from both sides to make sure you leave no streaks, and you'll always have happy customers. Before you leave, ask your customer to check your work to be sure you haven't forgotten a window.

Keep a notebook with the names, addresses, and telephone numbers of your customers and the date you last cleaned their windows. After three or four months have gone by, ask if they would like you to come back. Bet they'll say yes!

49

The Used Music Company

Here is a good way to turn old records and tapes into a dandy once-in-a-while business. Everyone who has a record player or tape deck has old records and tapes that they never listen to. Most people will be happy to have you take them away for nothing. You'll probably get a bunch of old children's records that have been outgrown, or old 45-rpm records that were popular years ago, or long-playing albums that are no longer needed. Classical, pop, rock, reggae, jazz, or western, records or tapes—there is usually someone who's looking for the very thing that someone else is throwing out.

Make the rounds of your neighborhood to collect records. Tell everyone who gives you some to come to your big sale. Give people a coupon for one free record or tape for every five they give you.

Pick a Saturday morning or afternoon for your sale. Be sure to advertise beforehand so that people can plan to be there. You could make posters to put up around your neighborhood several days ahead. Or have a parade with signs. You could make complimentary tickets and give them away free to tell people when and where the big sale is.

On the day of your sale, get a big table and put out all the records and tapes in boxes. Try dividing them into categories (children's, classical, and so on). Have a record player or radio playing music to put people into the mood to buy. (It will also attract customers.) List your big hits on a poster or blackboard. Sell 45s for 50¢, 33s (albums) for 75¢, and tapes for 75¢.

Be sure to have your sale in a place where people will see it. A garage right near the sidewalk is a good place. Have a big bowl of free popcorn and little cups of apple juice for 10¢ per cup to attract customers. There is nothing like refreshments and used music to put people in a buying mood.

Pay attention to the musicians that the people seem most interested in; then the next time you have a used-music sale, you'll know who to put at the top of your advertising posters.

The Saturday Matinee Escort Service

This is the job for you if you like to go to the movies and the theater. All you have to do is to keep an eye on the theater section of your local paper. Watch for announcements of movies, stage plays, puppet shows, or concerts that are especially for children. It shouldn't be hard to find customers. If you do babysitting, call your customers and offer to take their children and some of their friends to the Saturday matinee. You could put up a notice about your service at the grocery store or the library. If you are taking kids for whom you don't babysit, their parents may want to see a reference. Have one of your regular customers write a letter saying that you are good with younger children and very reliable.

Here are some things to think about.

1. When you decide which show you want to see, find out what age the movies will appeal to.

Don't take kids to something that's too old or too young for them. They'll be bored and restless.

2. Figure out how you will get there. It's great if you can walk, but you may have to make arrangements for a grown-up to drive you there. If you live in the city, you may have to take a bus. It's a good idea to take a test run beforehand so you'll be familiar with the route and any transfers you will need. Or you might consider taking a taxi. Find out how much it will cost, including a tip, and figure that into your expenses.

3. Decide how many kids you can take. Take only two or three until you get the hang of it. *Never* take more children than you can keep a careful watch over, especially if you are using public transportation.

4. It is a good idea to buy your tickets ahead of time for concerts and stage plays. If you do, get the money from the parents beforehand and tell them that it is not refundable if they cancel at the last minute.

5. Figure out what your expenses will be and add them to the price of your babysitting time to determine how much to charge for your escort service. Don't forget to include the price of your own ticket. You might want to figure in the cost of some refreshments, like a bucket of popcorn for each kid.

51

The Gopher Errand Service

When you run errands, you're a "gopher." You go fer groceries. You go fer the newspapers. You go fer something at the drugstore or bakery. Of course, if you're not fond of gophers, you could call your service The Greased-Lightning Errand Service or The Speeding-Bullet Errand Service or whatever you like.

First, make yourself a symbol. Every errand service needs a symbol. Here are a few ideas.

RABBIT TRANSIT
SPEEDING ROCKET
SPINNIN' WHEELS
GREASED LIGHTNING
Streakin' Sneaks
ACK!

Next, make some announcements that you can take around to neighbors and friends. Be sure to put your symbol on them. (You could also put it on your bike and on a T-shirt to help advertise your service.)

Your announcement might be something like this one.

RAIN-OR-SHINE ERRAND SERVICE
THE NEXT TIME YOU FORGET
SOMETHING AT THE STORE, DON'T
DRIVE BACK FOR IT.
CALL: GRETCHEN HUMPHREY
PHONE: 774-4546
I will get it for you on my bike.
ANYTHING that will fit in my bike basket
can be delivered to your door in a few
minutes.
Afternoons, 3:00-5:00
Saturdays, 10:00-5:00

How to Charge

Try to keep your fees small. Fifty cents for short trips. One dollar for long ones or two trips. Here is an example.

Mrs. Findley calls and tells you that she'd like you to go to the pet store and get her a pound of liver for her cat. First, you have to go to Mrs. Findley's place to pick up the money (50¢). Then you have to go to the store and buy the liver. Finally you bring it back to Mrs. Findley (50¢, or a total of $1.00). If Mrs. Findley lives a long way from you, and the pet store is a long way from Mrs. Findley, then you should charge more for each trip.

Here are some things to think about for an errand business.

1. Be dependable. If you advertise that your service is available every day, then you have to do it every day. Start with Saturdays only, or just a couple of afternoons (the same ones) each week.

2. Think about who needs your service most. People who don't have cars. People who sell small things that you can carry easily. Old people who have trouble getting out regularly. If there's a retirement home in your community, that would be a good place to put up a small poster. Be sure that the right kinds of people get to know about your service.

3. Be patient. It will take some time for people to learn about your new service. Then it will take a while for them to learn that they can count on you. You'll have to advertise regularly at first, but pretty soon you'll get regular customers.

4. After you've been in business for a while, go to the drugstore and tell the druggist that you would like to deliver for him too. Try the same thing with other stores. Ask one of your regular customers to write a recommendation that you can show to the storekeepers.

Used Books and Comics Sale and Exchange

A book sale can be run the same way as a record sale. Gather books around the neighborhood. On the day of the sale, put them out in boxes. Arrange the books so that the titles show. Children's books should be in one place and adult books in another. Separate fiction from nonfiction, and sort them into boxes by price. You will probably have mostly paperback books, but if you get some hardcover books that are in good condition, you might want to display them separately on card tables.

Here are some suggestions about what to charge.

Regular paperbacks .... 10¢
Large-format paperbacks .... 25¢
Children's, small cardboard cover .... 10¢
Children's, large picture .... 25¢
Comic books ....5¢

Hardcover books should be priced from 25¢ to $3.00, depending on their condition and contents. You might want to get a grown-up friend who knows a lot about books to help you decide on prices. Write the prices in pencil on the first page.

If you want to run an exchange, tell people they can select one of your books in exchange for two of theirs of the same value.

As a sideline, set up a table where you sell paperback-book covers and fancy bookmarks. Make a poster to advertise your wares.

Paperback-Book Covers

These aren't hard to make and are a wonderful way to refurbish old paperbacks that you want to keep on your bookshelf.

You Will Need
cardboard (noncorrugated)
fabric scraps
fancy wrapping paper
white glue
metal ruler
razor knife
old paintbrush
scissors
lots of newspapers to work on

CLOTH COVERS

1. Measure a typical paperbook book. It will be about 7 ¼ inches by 4¼ inches. Cut two pieces of cardboard (one for the front and one for the back cover) slightly larger than the dimensions of the book, or about 7½ inches by 4½ inches.

2. Now measure the backs, or spines, of several books. You can see that there are many different widths, depending on how long the story is. For your first cover, select one that is pretty average, say, one that measures about ¾ inch thick. Cut a piece of cardboard for the spine of your cover that measures 1 inch by 7½ inches. So, you see, you have added about ¼ inch to each measurement so that the cover will be slightly larger than the book itself.

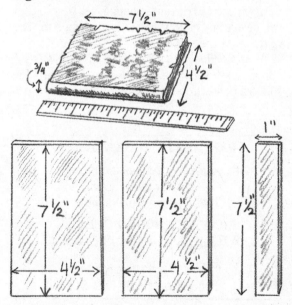

3. Lay your cardboard pieces on the wrong side of a length of pretty fabric. Line them up carefully on the straight grain of the fabric, leaving a gap of about ⅛ inch on each side of the spine, between the front and back pieces. Draw lightly with a pencil around the edges of the cardboard. Cut the fabric to size, adding an extra inch on all four sides.

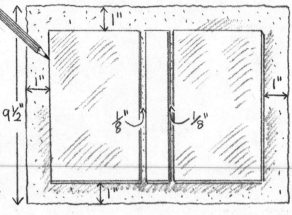

4. Brush one side of the cardboard pieces with a thin layer of glue and place them inside the pencil outlines. Glue down the corners, then the excess fabric all the way around. Set aside to dry.

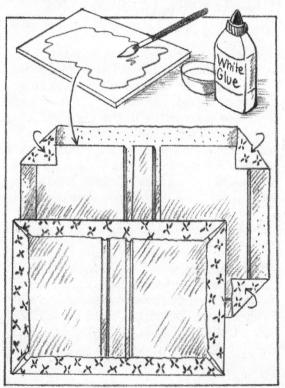

5. Measure the length and width of the cover you just made. Cut a piece of fancy lining paper (gift wrapping is good) that measures ¾ inch more than the cover from top to bottom and 11 inches more than the width. This will be about 7¼ inches by 21 inches for your sample cover.

6. Mark with a pencil on the wrong side of the lining paper a ½ inch border all the way around.

Make two lines 2 ½ inches apart on each side, as shown in the diagram. Fold the paper along all the lines to make 2 ½-inch pockets on both sides. Then fold under the ½-inch border all the way around, like a hem. Glue the hem in place on the wrong side, being careful not to get any glue on the front of the lining or in the pockets. Brush the inside of the cover with a thin layer of glue, and glue the lining in place.

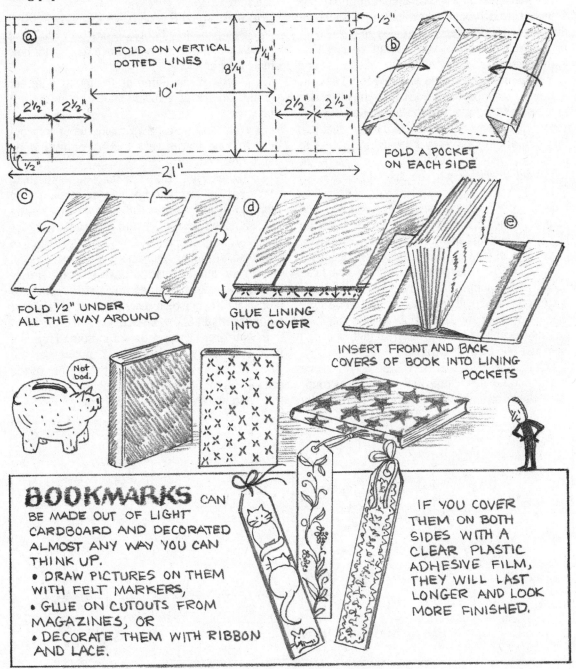

(a) FOLD ON VERTICAL DOTTED LINES
7¼"
8¼"
10"
2½" 2½"
2½" 2½"
½"
½"
21"

(b) ½"
FOLD A POCKET ON EACH SIDE

(c) FOLD ½" UNDER ALL THE WAY AROUND

(d) GLUE LINING INTO COVER

(e) INSERT FRONT AND BACK COVERS OF BOOK INTO LINING POCKETS

Not bad.

BOOKMARKS CAN BE MADE OUT OF LIGHT CARDBOARD AND DECORATED ALMOST ANY WAY YOU CAN THINK UP.
• DRAW PICTURES ON THEM WITH FELT MARKERS,
• GLUE ON CUTOUTS FROM MAGAZINES, OR
• DECORATE THEM WITH RIBBON AND LACE.

IF YOU COVER THEM ON BOTH SIDES WITH A CLEAR PLASTIC ADHESIVE FILM, THEY WILL LAST LONGER AND LOOK MORE FINISHED.

Master's Sport and Study Clinic

Are you especially good at something? Are you a master hand at baseball or knitting or tennis or drawing? Do you get top grades in French or math? Well, if you do, you can put your skill or knowledge to work earning money and helping someone else at the same time. Become a tutor.

Being a tutor probably doesn't sound like much fun, neither to you nor to the tutee, so call yourself a helper or just a friend. No matter what it is that you are going to teach, your first job is to figure out what you know that you can show or tell someone else. Try to think about how you got to be good at it.

Most people learn a new skill in steps. They start with one small part of the whole and then go on to another and another. So make yourself a game plan of how you are going to teach your skill. Decide whether you can teach two or three people at the same time or whether it will work better one on one. If you are teaching something that takes a lot of concentration, like math or playing the guitar, you'll probably find it easier to have just one pupil at a time.

Other skills lend themselves better to group instruction. Some children learn faster in a group, and others are more comfortable learning by themselves. These are all things that you will have to think about and decide for yourself.

The other thing you will have to decide is how much to charge for your service. You can charge more for one-on-one tutoring than you can for group instruction. One important thing to keep in mind is that you'll be a success as a tutor only if you get results, that is, if you can actually teach people something or make them a little better than they were.

Here are some tips on teaching.

1. Be patient. People learn at different speeds, and it doesn't have much to do with how smart they are.

2. Words mean different things to different people, so try to explain things in more than one way.

3. *Never* use sarcasm or make fun of your pupils. No one learns very quickly or well when being ridiculed.

4. Make it fun. If you're teaching something that's sort of dry, like spelling or math, try to think up ways to make it into a game.

It shouldn't be too hard to find customers for your tutoring business. If you are planning to teach an academic subject, put up notices on school and library bulletin boards. State clearly what age and level of student you are prepared to help. Talk to your own teacher about your plans; he or she might know of someone you could help.

If your area of expertise is in something like sports or crafts or dance, post notices at the YMCA and YWCA, community center, grade school, recreation center, or anywhere kids and their parents are likely to see them.

The Organization Organization

Some people are naturally tidy and love to organize things. If you're one of them, offer to sort it out for those other people who'd like to be in alphabetical order but hate to do it. Distribute flyers around your neighborhood and see what interesting jobs come your way.

On-the-Spot Car Washing

This is a job that you can do by yourself, but it's a lot more fun to do it with a friend. Start a car-washing business. You can keep it very simple and just wash the outside of cars. For a little more money, you can offer to clean the inside as well. If you want to work harder and make even more money, you can go into the polishing and waxing business.

THE OUTSIDE

You Will Need (for washing only)
  bucket
  mild liquid soap or commercial car-washing soap
  brush with stiff bristles (not wire)
  cleansing powder or commercial tire cleaner
  sponge or replacement head for a string mop
  clean rags or chamois cloth
  household glass cleaner

Never wash a car in the bright sun or when the metal is hot. It will dry too fast and leave soap and water spots. Start by hosing the car all over, even underneath. Fill a bucket with cold water and a mild liquid soap. (Don't use detergent. It will remove the wax and bleach the paint.) If the car is very dirty, you may want to use a commercial car-washing soap. With a sponge or mop head, scrub one small section at a time, starting with the roof. Rinse the soap off as you go so it doesn't dry and cause streaks and spots. Scrub the tires with a stiff brush (not a wire one), and if necessary scour them with powdered cleanser or a commercial tire cleaner. Don't ever use a petroleum product such as kerosene or gasoline because it will eat into the rubber. When you have washed the entire car (you may have to do it twice), hose it down again and then quickly dry it with soft rags or, better still, a chamois. Clean the windows and rearview mirrors with a household glass cleaner.

THE INSIDE

If you want to extend your car-washing service to include cleaning the interiors, you'll have to bring some additional supplies.

You Will Need
household spray cleaner
spray polish or a commercial
    protective coating
whiskbroom and dustpan or vacuum
    cleaner
clean rags
small trash bags for cars

The first step when cleaning the interior of a car is to turn off the ceiling light so it doesn't run down the battery while the doors are open. Empty the ashtrays and wipe them out with a damp rag. Take out the floor mats, scrub them with soap and water and lay them out to dry. Then, starting with the ceiling, spray a small amount of cleaner on the vinyl and wipe it with a soft, clean cloth. You can use the spray on all plastic and vinyl surfaces. Use it sparingly so it doesn't drip or soak into seams. Don't use it on fabric seats. They should be brushed with a whisk-broom or vacuumed. When everything is clean, apply some protective polish to the door panels, the dashboard, and the back deck. Clean the inside of the windows with window cleaner. Don't forget to do the rearview mirror. Brush or vacuum the carpets and replace the mats when they are dry. If the car does not have one of those little hanging trash bags, you might put one in as a special service. You can probably get some free from AAA or a local conservation group.

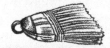

POLISHING & WAXING

Polishing and waxing are much harder work than just washing, and require some skill. You should probably try doing your car or a friend's at least once before you decide whether you really want to get into it. If you have a grown-up friend who has an old car that is starting to look dull, ask if you can practice on it. If you decide to go ahead with the project:

You Will Need
commercial car polish
liquid and paste wax
chrome polish
vinyl-top restorer
lots and lots of clean rags

It's easy to tell when a car needs to be waxed. First, spray it with water. If the water collects in round beads, it's okay as it is. If the water spreads, you know it needs wax. If the car is fairly new and the finish is still shiny and in good condition, all it will need is waxing. Always wax a car in the shade.

There are two kinds of car wax: paste and liquid. Liquid wax is applied with a soft, dry cloth. Apply it to one small section of the car at a time, rubbing it on with an overlapping circular motion. Let the wax dry until it turns chalky and there are no damp spots, then buff it with a clean cloth, using the same circular motion. Every so often, refold your cloth to expose a fresh surface. Paste wax is applied in the same way but with a damp cloth. Don't try to do too large a portion at once. Buff the area well before moving on to the next portion.

A car that needs to be polished looks dull because the paint has begun to deteriorate and turn cloudy. Polishing removes the layer of oxidized paint and leaves a fresh unprotected paint surface which needs to be waxed. So if you polish a car, it must be waxed as well. The polish is used in much the same way as liquid wax, but it requires a little more elbow grease. Again, do only a small section of the car at a time, and polish it with clean rags. When you have done the entire car, give it a good coat of paste wax. It's always a good idea to use paste wax after polishing as it gives a more durable finish than liquid wax. If the car has a vinyl top, it can be treated with a commercial restorer. Some of them require buffing, others do not. Use liquid chrome polish on bumpers and trim.

It should be fairly easy to find customers. To start, just ask around your neighborhood. The weekend is a good time, when people are outside and working around in their yards. Introduce yourself and tell them about your business. You might have a printed flyer telling about what you are prepared to do and giving prices for each service.

ON-THE-SPOT CAR WASHING
Joe Smith and Jenny Brown announce the
opening of their new business.
We will wash, clean, polish, and wax your car
at your own home.

WASH $3.00
CLEAN INTERIOR $2.50
POLISH $10.00
LIQUID WAX $6.00
PASTE WAX $8.00
Call Joe: 446-7845
Call Jenny: 446-9432
Weekend appointments only

If you can't find enough work in your neighborhood, put up notices at the supermarket or laundromat. Ask if you can post a flyer at the local gas station or garage, if they don't offer a washing service.

You can expand your service and create goodwill by doing some extras. Check the tire pressure, oil, and water and let people know if they are low. Check the windshield-cleaner reservoir and fill it, if necessary.

Since your supplies will be fairly expensive, it would be smart to start up your business slowly. At first, do only washing and interior cleaning. When you have made some money doing that and are very sure that you want to expand your services, then buy your polishing and waxing supplies.

SPECIALTIMERS

There most likely isn't anyone in the world who knows better than you do what a kid's birthday party should be like. If you like birthdays, and if you like little kids, this might be just the right idea for you: start your own Happy-Birthday-Party Company.

Getting started is the hardest part. The best way is to go into it with a friend, so you'll have some help. Start by doing the first party free. Pick out some little kid you like and tell his or her mom and dad that you want to give a party as a present. If it works and everyone has a good time, ask those parents to tell their friends about your new business. Pretty soon word will get around.

A Party Plan

A good birthday party doesn't just *happen*. It's planned in advance. All the parts are considered and decided upon before they happen. That's important. Be sure to have a talk with the parents several days before each party. To start with, let parents take care of refreshments and party favors, if any. That way you can concentrate on the other parts. Here is a sample birthday-party schedule. (When you do a real one, it may be different. This one is just to give you the idea.)

SAMPLE BIRTHDAY SCHEDULE (when lunch is included)	
10:00	go to the birthday house and get set up
11:00	kids arrive and get their hats
11:15	active game 1
11:30	active game 2
11:45	quiet game, or presents
12:00	eat lunch: hot dogs, chips, carrot sticks, punch, cake, ice cream
12:30	puppet show or other entertainment
1:00	time to go home
1:00–1:30	cleanup time

Getting Organized

A birthday-party company needs lots of style. In a way, when you put on a party, you are putting on a grand show in which every person has a part. That's why birthday-party-goers get funny hats to wear. That's why you and your worker-friends may want to wear costumes. Here are some ideas for costumes that are simple to make and comfortable to wear.

For a clown shirt, take an old T-shirt. Paint a design on it with fabric paints or felt markers. Sew on scraps of bright fabric or old scarves.

To make a goofy yarn wig, make a cap out of an old stocking with the end tied and cut off. Get a ball of thick, bright-colored yarn and sew lengths of it all over the cap.

Paint your face with theatrical makeup. A mask would be too hot and stuffy to wear through a whole party.

Find some suspenders to hold up the baggy pants you make from some of your dad's old pajama bottoms. Cut them off and gather them with ribbons just above your knees.

Stuff some big garden gloves with newspaper and sew them to the top of an old shower cap or any cap you like.

Stuff the toes of some big men's socks with cotton and sew on a couple of pompoms or chunky buttons.

Be on the lookout for scraps of material, old sheets, socks, stockings, pantyhose, shower caps, junk jewelry, yarn, coats, buttons, pajamas, ribbons, T-shirts, pants, scarves, gloves, and so on.

Until you've had a dry run or two and know what you're doing, charge nothing. After that, you should probably get $8.00 to $10.00 for a two-hour party for up to ten kids. Charge more if the party is especially big or complicated, less if the parents want to handle decorations as well as food.

Discuss your plans with the grown-ups. Write out your plan for the party and show it to them in advance. List all the activities so they'll know what you need from them (chairs, tables, balls, or other props) and so you'll know what you need to bring from home. Make sure that you know whether or not there will be presents so you can allow time for opening them. (Some parents prefer parties without gifts.) Be sure you have the name of everyone who is coming. This discussion with the grown-ups is very important. Don't put it off.

Decorations

They are pretty important, because they make any place—indoors or out—*look* like a birthday party. But each place is quite different, and you'll have to decide with the grown-ups who will do what. Here are some ideas for simple decorations that look nice and don't cost much.

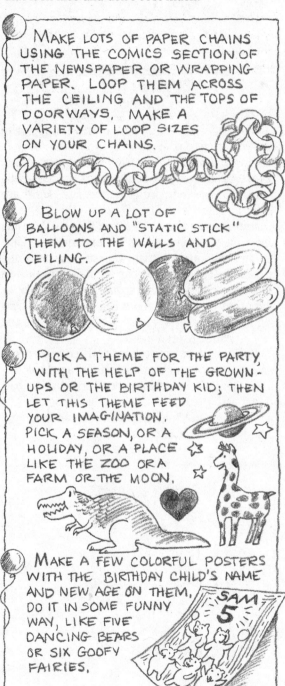

MAKE LOTS OF PAPER CHAINS USING THE COMICS SECTION OF THE NEWSPAPER OR WRAPPING PAPER. LOOP THEM ACROSS THE CEILING AND THE TOPS OF DOORWAYS. MAKE A VARIETY OF LOOP SIZES ON YOUR CHAINS.

BLOW UP A LOT OF BALLOONS AND "STATIC STICK" THEM TO THE WALLS AND CEILING.

PICK A THEME FOR THE PARTY WITH THE HELP OF THE GROWN-UPS OR THE BIRTHDAY KID; THEN LET THIS THEME FEED YOUR IMAGINATION. PICK A SEASON, OR A HOLIDAY, OR A PLACE LIKE THE ZOO OR A FARM OR THE MOON.

MAKE A FEW COLORFUL POSTERS WITH THE BIRTHDAY CHILD'S NAME AND NEW AGE ON THEM. DO IT IN SOME FUNNY WAY, LIKE FIVE DANCING BEARS OR SIX GOOFY FAIRIES.

SAM 5

10:00: Getting ready. Get there at least a half-hour in advance. Check to be sure everything is ready. Put up any decorations that you are responsible for. Set up any chairs and tables that you will need for activities. Be sure to remove anything that might get broken or knocked over accidentally. Put the party hats where you want them.

11:00: Everybody comes. Most little kids aren't late for birthday parties unless some grown-up makes them late. So be ready on time. Be ready to keep them busy from the very start. Here are a couple of good ways to do that.

Find Your Hat. Print each guest's name on a party hat. Hang the hats from the ceiling if you can do it easily. Or put them around the room in funny places. Make sure you have a spare blank one and a felt marker around just in case an extra person shows up at the last minute. Everyone finds his or her hat and puts it on.

Getting-acquainted game: Simon Sez. This game is a good one to begin with because it gets the party started right off and introduces you (or you and your friend) as the party clown, or whatever. It's easy and fun. Most kids already know how to play it, people can join in as they arrive, and it can go on as long as you want.

You play the part of Simon and tell the kids what to do. Besides the usual things such as, Simon sez, "Put your hands on your head," you could include some actions with a birthday theme. Try Simon sez, "Blow out the candles," or "Point to the birthday girl," or "Eat a piece of cake."

11:15: The first game. Plan one or two active games and a quiet one to finish up with. This way the kids will have a chance to calm down before refreshments or lunch. Here are two lively games that take about ten or fifteen minutes to play.

Feather Blow. You need enough kids for at least two teams of four each. The team holds hands in a circle, and one person (the birthday kid on her team) starts by blowing the feather into the air. Everyone tries to keep it floating just by blowing (no hands). The team that keeps it up longest wins. Use a little, light feather, like the kind from a pillow.

Under the Bridge. Everyone stands in a circle with legs apart and feet touching the next kid's. You need eight or ten kids, with the birthday kid in the center to start. She has a big rubber ball and tries to roll it through the legs of the other players, the "bridges." Everyone tries to keep the ball away, using only hands. If the ball rolls through someone's legs, then that person is "it."

11:30: The second game. If the first game hasn't tired everyone out, or taken too much time, play another pretty active one. Here are two more.

Peanut Race. Divide the group into two teams and have them line up behind one another. Give the first kid on each team a plastic teaspoon and a peanut. The object is for each child in turn to carry the peanut in the spoon around a chair at the other end of the room and back to the next kid in line, until the entire team has carried the peanut. First team done wins.

Balloon Race. Line the kids up in two teams as you did for the last game. This time, however, have them take a balloon around the chair by batting it with their hands, blowing it, or kicking it— anything *but* holding it in their hands and running. The team that finishes first wins.

11:45: Quiet game (or birthday presents). If this is a party with presents, this might be a good time to open them. If not, try a quiet game to slow things down a bit before it is time to eat refreshments or lunch. Everyone sits in a circle.

I'm Thinking of a Color. The birthday child starts by picking out an object in the room and telling only what color it is, red, for instance. Everyone takes turns guessing the red things in the room, and the first one to guess the right object gets to pick the next object.

Tell a story. Make up a silly story that has lots of characters, and assign one to each kid. The characters don't all have to be people, they can be animals or cars or the wind or a tree. Whenever you mention someone's character while telling the story, that person gets to make a special sound (like beep-beep or whooosh or cock-a-doodle-doo). Make sure that everyone's character is mentioned at least three times.

12:00: Lunchtime. While the kids are eating, you can be getting organized for the entertainment that follows.

12:30: The grand finale. Now it's time for you to put on your show. It can be a puppet show, or it could be a bunch of magic tricks. Here are some ideas for a simple puppet show that little kids will like.

Look at *The Saturday Sometimes Puppet Palace* in this book for how to make a puppet stage, but if you want something simpler, just put a bright cloth over a card table and sit behind it so both you and the puppets are visible. Following is a magic trick that introduces two puppets: a rabbit and a magician. Afterward you could have the puppets do silly things to you or to each other, such as playing tricks on you which the audience gets but you pretend not to. Or use the puppets to teach a song. Anyway, keep it short and simple, about fifteen minutes or less.

1. Put a hat upside down on the back edge of your table. Have the rabbit show the audience that it's empty.

2. Flip the hat over and put it just over the back edge of the table. Now comes the trick! With your free hand quickly sneak the magician puppet, all rolled up, inside the hat and then turn the hat back over.

3. Unwrap the magician by having the rabbit look for him inside the hat.

65

4. Next, explain to the rabbit that the only way to pull a magician out of a hat is for some special person to say the magic words "Pretty please."

5. Get everyone in the audience to take turns saying "Pretty please!" Last of all, have the birthday kid say it and then, Wonder of Wonders! This time when the rabbit reaches inside the hat, he pulls out a magician!

And then it's time to go home (except for you).

1:00–1:30: Cleanup time. Birthday parties are pretty messy affairs. Help your customer by sticking around for a half-hour or so to clean up. At the very least, clean up your own things. Take down the decorations. Replace moved furniture. Collect your own costumes and props. If you want to make a big hit, help clear the table and wash up the dishes.

SOMETHING TO REMEMBER

KEEP IN MIND THAT ALTHOUGH **YOU** ARE PUTTING ON A **SHOW** AND ORGANIZING THE **PARTY**, YOU ARE DOING IT FOR The Birthday Child. BE SURE THAT IT IS *HIS* OR *HER* SHOW TOO. THROUGHOUT THE PARTY, TRY TO THINK OF WAYS TO MAKE THE BIRTHDAY CHILD THE CENTER OF ATTENTION FOR A FEW MINUTES.

ALINA'S BIRTHDAY-PARTY SERVICE

Alina Meneken is eleven years old. She manages birthday parties for little kids. Alina got started in business when she organized a party for her younger sister. The mother of one of the birthday guests was so impressed that she asked Alina to do a party for her child. Alina doesn't provide or prepare the refreshments; she just organizes the games and supervises the children while the grown-ups have their own party in another room. Ahead of time she decides which games to play and tells the parents what supplies she will need. Alina charges from $10.00 to $12.00 for a party, depending on how long it goes on and how many kids are invited.

We've all dyed eggs since we were toddlers—pink, blue, and yellow eggs. Would you like to create eggs so beautiful that you could sell them? Here are a few new ways to liven up your Easter basket.

Crayon resist. These are fun and would be a good way to make personalized eggs with people's names on them. First, make up some red, yellow, and blue food-coloring dye. Use the recipe on the box, and let the dye cool to room temperature.

Plan a pattern or picture in your mind that you want on your egg, or for the first one just experiment and see what happens. Sharpen a crayon (any color) in a pencil sharpener or with a knife. Draw something on the egg with the crayon, or write a name. What you have just drawn will turn out to be white, even though it doesn't look that way now.

Next, dip the egg in the yellow dye. Dry it and draw something more on the egg. What you have just drawn will turn out to be yellow.

Now dip the egg into the red dye until it is a rosy pink. Take it out, dry it, and cover whatever you want to remain pink with crayon lines.

Finally, dip the egg into the blue dye. Leave it until it is a pretty deep purplish blue. Take it out and dry it. Polish it very gently with a soft rag that has been warmed in the oven. The crayon wax will come off on the rag and BEHOLD! a marvelous multicolored egg!

Onion-skin eggs. Strip all the brown or red papery skin off some onions. Or ask the grocer to save you some. You don't need very many; about two cupfuls will do. Put them in a saucepan with about three cups of water and boil them until the water turns brown, about twenty minutes.

Gather some pretty, feathery leaves and ferns, ones that have an interesting outline. Some simple flowers will work if they are not too thick. Soak them in water until they are rather limp.

Lay a leaf or flower on an egg. If you want, you can make up a very thin mixture of water and white glue to stick the leaves to the eggs. Wrap the egg tightly with cheesecloth to hold the plant in place and boil the egg in onion water for ten minutes. Remove and unwrap the egg. Polish it with a little dab of butter to make it shiny.

Tissue-paper eggs. Paint the egg all over with a thin solution of water and white glue. Tear up some little pieces of colored tissue paper. The brightest colors work best. Stick them every which way all over the egg. Paint over them with the glue mixture. Let the egg sit for a couple of minutes and then remove the paper. Your egg will come out a beautiful motley mottle of colors.

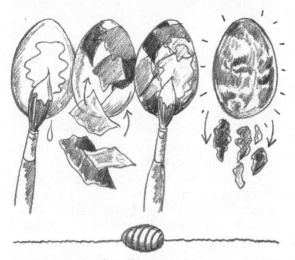

Blown eggs. You know how to blow an egg, don't you? You prick a small hole in the little end and a slightly larger one in the big end and then blow through the small hole until all the insides come out the big one. Well, once you've blown out the eggs and washed them and let them dry, you can do all sorts of things with them. You can make personalized, crayon-resist eggs or any other kind you want. The advantage to blown eggs is that they can be kept from one Easter to the next. But there are some other things you can do with them that are fun.

SMALL HOLE

SLIGHTLY LARGER HOLE

Candy eggs. Blow and decorate the eggs any way you wish. For candy eggs you should make the bottom hole quite large, about as big around as a nickel. This makes blowing them a lot easier. Fill the finished eggs with small candies. Seal the hole with gold paper seals.

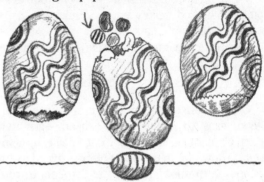

Confetti eggs. Make the eggs the same way you made the candy eggs, but fill them with confetti. These are fun for parties because when you throw them, all the confetti comes flying out. You could decorate the eggs by painting them with glue and rolling them in glittery confetti.

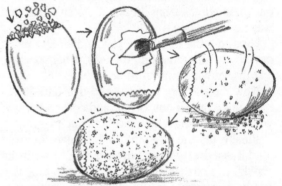

Blown eggs are the only ones that are practical to try to sell. Collect eggshells all year. Every time someone in your house is going to make something that uses eggs, ask if you can blow them for the shells. If you know a farmer who raises ducks, see if you can get some duck eggs to blow. Make some samples of your eggs and take them to gift shops and variety stores. Tell them that you will take orders for personalized eggs. Sell your eggs to the store for 25¢ for regular ones and 50¢ for duck eggs or personalized eggs. The store will probably mark the prices up to 50¢ and 75¢ to make a profit.

Out in La Cañada, California (that's near Los Angeles), there is a boy who is so crazy about Halloween that every year he and his friends put on a big show. Their show is a big attraction, and each year it gets a little better. Maybe Chuck's show will give you ideas about one of your own.

This year's show was in Rodney White's yard, where there is a real creek with flowing water. Their theme was gold mining, and they had a sluice box, a gold-mining pan, and other stuff. They even brought a dead tree from Devil's Gate Dam and set it up. Lots of people came to see the show, which Chuck calls The Halloween Scene.

Chuck had help with his show. Here he is (on the left) with two helpers. Bob (Chuck's older brother) is in the middle, and Rodney White is on the other side. Bob is holding their credits board. Bruce Norquist also helped.

Here is Bob in his costume in front of a miner's shack, which Chuck and his helpers built from scratch. Notice the Restricted sign and other man-made junk. There is even a skull—can you see it?

69

THE HALLOWEEN SCENE
by Chuck McClain

Our Halloween scene was made by my brother Bob, Bruce Norquist, Rodney White, and me. It was at Rodney White's house. It was in his side yard.

We got the idea for a Halloween scene about February. Then we decided to make it a gold-mining town.

We started planning it in March of last year. We drove around Foothill Boulevard looking for old bottles, rusted cans, pots, dead branches, and tumbleweeds for good special effects. We went to the library and got books on ghost towns and mining camps. On my birthday we went to Knott's Berry Farm and studied their ghost town and mine. There, we bought some documents, a Wanted poster, and a gold-mining pan. We worked hard on collecting stuff all year.

We started working on it about September 22. I made a schedule of jobs for each person. The most complicated things we made were a gold mine, a miner's shack, and a river. The mine we made was in the White's cellar. We had it boarded up. Then there was a stairway down to a doorway which had ripped-up sheets moving because we had a fan on them. Behind the fan was a red floodlight to make it look like a fire was down in the mine.

The miner's shack was made of old boards and some plywood. It had one window and a wrecked door and a broken roof that had a branch through it.

The river had running water through it. The water ran down under a wall, into a sluice box, and into a hole. The river branched off at the sluice box and went under a walkway down into the street.

Some other things in the scene we had to make and get were a dead tree from Devil's Gate Dam. And then we made a tent of a miner that had a candle in it. Then by the tent was a cross and a grave.

In the scene we had about seven floodlights. Bob did most of the electricity work. On the Halloween scene we had a record of sound effects playing very loud. The admission was 10¢ for each person. It was a great success, and it was very fun. We hope to do another one this year. It is important to get some publicity in the newspaper so people will know where to go.

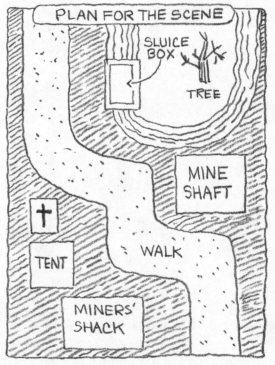

PLAN FOR THE SCENE

SLUICE BOX

TREE

MINE SHAFT

WALK

TENT

MINERS' SHACK

Goblin Garment Manufacturer

Collect materials in advance, so by October 1 you are ready to begin.

You Will Need
- paper bags
- boxes
- cardboard tubes
- shirt cardboard
- yarn
- colored paper
- funny papers
- felt markers
- poster paint
- white glue
- tape
- wrapping paper
- ribbons
- paper plates
- old sheets
- inexpensive fabrics
- scissors

Did you know there are a lot of people who hate to buy their kids those tacky Halloween costumes that are sold in stores? They're dumb looking and expensive, but if people don't know how to sew or don't have time to make costumes, they don't have any choice. You could provide another choice and put some change in your pockets. Sit down with a pencil and paper and draw designs for some weird, funny costumes. What did you draw? A cross-eyed, kinky-tailed cat? A fairy princess with a nose like Groucho Marx? A hobo that looks like a patchwork doll? A pumpkin that looks like it needs an orthodontist? Now that you've got the spooky spirit, you are ready to be a goblin garment manufacturer.

Make a sample batch of costumes and take them around your neighborhood, or put on a goblin fashion show in your garage several weeks before Halloween. Decorate the garage to fit the occasion. Be ready to take orders in advance. Charge $4.00 to $6.00 for each costume, depending on how much it costs you for supplies and how long it takes to make a costume. If you keep your costumes simple and funny, you'll do a terrific business. And you'll make Halloween a little bit weirder.

①

This mask is made from a paper plate, with holes for eyes and paper ears and glued-on whiskers. It has holes punched in the sides with a string running through them to hold it in. It is painted with poster paints.

②

This costume is just a piece of old sheet or a big piece of fabric folded in half, with a hole cut in the center for your head. You could paint crazy designs on it or sew patches of bright material. The tail is a piece of rope, painted and sewn on the back.

③

This mask is made from a paper bag, with the corners clipped off and taped shut. There are bright strips of colored paper glued on for hair and eyes; the teeth are aluminum foil; holes have been cut for seeing and breathing.

④

This creature is made from a corrugated cardboard box with holes cut in the sides for arms and head. It has cardboard tubes taped on and a small cardboard box with peculiar knobs and dials painted on it. What else can you think of to add to this costume?

⑤

This costume has a papier-mâché mask, with holes punched in the front for eyes, and with smaller holes along the edge, where yarn has been threaded through for hair. The mask shape is made by wrapping newspaper strips that have been soaked in a mixture of white glue and water (half and half) around one half of a blown-up balloon. When it's dry, pop the balloon, cut out the eyes, and paint the mask.

⑥

This costume is made the way the first one was, only the bottom is cut in a zigzag. The big floppy collar is made of funny papers glued together in a big circle. Cut a hole in the center large enough for your head.

The Jack-O'-Lantern Kids

You won't find a pumpkin patch in New York City, or in Chicago, or in any other big city. So if you live in one of those places, you can start a Halloween business that will bring a little cheer to all the people who never get to see a pumpkin patch, and who might not have a jack-o'-lantern if you don't come around.

First, you'll have to make arrangements with a grocer. Find a friendly one and explain your plan to take orders for Halloween pumpkins and say that you'll buy all your pumpkins from that store if he or she will give you a special price.

Where we live, pumpkins are plentiful. They cost about 10¢ per pound. That means a 5-pounder goes for 50¢. Maybe your grocer will get

them for you at 10¢ per pound, and you can sell them for 15¢ to 18¢ per pound. The amount you make pays for your time in taking orders and delivering. After you make arrangements with the grocer, make the rounds of the neighborhood. Make two display cards to take around. One should show pumpkin sizes and estimated prices. Ask your customer to pick the size they want. Tell them that the prices are only approximate because you will charge by the pound.

Then show them your other card. On it you will have drawn as many pumpkin faces as you can think of. (Be sure they are simple enough to actually cut in a pumpkin.) Tell your customers, that for $2.00 extra, you will carve their pumpkins and provide a candle. Write the orders down in your order book. Be sure to put down what size each person wants.

When the pumpkins arrive, get the grocer to weigh and mark each one, so you'll know how much to charge. Deliver them the afternoon of the day before Halloween at the latest. Do it the day before that if you can. If you save all the seeds from the jacks, you can roast them and take them around to sell too!

SPOOK HOUSE

Here is a fine and terrible idea. You can use your weirdest, craziest, niftiest tricks (so long as they don't hurt anyone) to scare people. You can be an architect, carpenter, artist, monster-maker, and freak-show organizer all in one. Then you can collect money from people who come to be scared out of their T-shirts in your bone-shaking, spine-chilling, brain-staggering, wailing, shrieking, hysterical, disgusting spook house.

The idea behind this show is to take people through a darkened space and to surprise them with whatever you can think of that will be scary and weird, *but in no way harmful or dangerous*. It should be dark, so people can't get a good look at how your tricks work, but it should not be so dark that people crash about and can't find their way. (Also, if it's too dark, little kids won't go in at all, and that's bad for business.)

Most important, there must be no nails or splinters to poke people, or greasy things that could stain clothes, or anything that could spoil someone's scary, good time. (Besides, you don't want to spend all the money you make paying to have someone's clothes cleaned or someone's hand stitched up, do you? I didn't think so.)

Where to Have a Spook House

A spook house can be anywhere. You could do it outdoors if you can get enough tents or huge boxes. You could make any garage into a first-class spook house. Or you could do it in a basement, or even in an alley (one that isn't used by cars).

There are three important design features for any high-quality spook house. First, it is one way only. Traffic goes through in one direction. (That means you need an entrance *and* an exit.) Second, it should be divided into different spaces (like little rooms) where different things happen. You can do that by turning corners, or by having openings from one space to another. Third, it is darkened (but not pitch black). Anyplace you can create those three conditions is a good place for a spook house.

Things that are good for building spook houses.....

Here are some things that are good to have available when you begin building your spook house.

1. Old sheets and blankets. The more the better. They enclose space. They help to contain sound (so people can't hear what's coming next). Sheets can be dyed spooky colors and hung in front of light bulbs to make a weird, colored space. (Be sure it's okay with your parents before you begin dyeing.) Or sheets can be torn into strips that hang down in the face and feel icky.

2. Big cardboard boxes. The kind refrigerators come in. They make good "spook rooms." Especially if your spook house is outside. Just be sure that they are anchored to the ground securely so someone doesn't accidentally knock one over.

3. Tents. All kinds: pup tents, two-man tents, family sizes.

4. Tarps and parachutes. Anything your folks might have around that covers something big (like a car or boat).

5. Big plastic sheets. Not the thin kind of plastic. The heavy green or black stuff that's used the same way a tarp is.

6. Folding screens, old doors, door frames. These can be used to make walls. Anything that is big enough for someone to walk under or through will work. (*Note*: Don't make doorways so small that people have to crawl or bend way over. It doesn't work.)

Things that are very SCARY...

Here are some ideas for the scariest of the scary.

1. Spirit lights. Get a string of those Christmas lights that blink and put them behind a blue or green cloth so they aren't bright. Or put blue cellophane over a flashlight; then hang it from the ceiling in a corner and push it to make it swing.

2. Ghoul hands. Rubber gloves half full of water and tied tightly at the end.

3. Spiders. Ones made of styrofoam or rubber, pipe cleaners, and black yarn.

4. Spider webs. Hanging thread.

5. Ghoul drool. Wet yarn or string.

6. Monster Breath. A fan blowing over some smelly cheese or a can of old cat food.

7. Shrunken heads. Papier-mâché heads with yarn hair, with nails sticking out of them, hung on springs so they bob up and down. (Or rubber ones from joke stores.)

8. Vampire. A kid dressed in black, with huge fangs, who drinks tomato juice from a clear glass bottle. Have a fake wooden stake through his heart and have him lie in a coffin. He can rear up and take a swig when people come in.

Sound effects.........

If you have a tape recorder, here are some things you could put on your sound effects tape to play during the walk.

1. Heavy breathing. Something not too loud, but constant and a little sinister, which builds up in volume. If you leave it on for a little while when people first come in, they will know that something scary is going to happen, and that will make it even scarier. Heavy breathing is great, and you could also try some kind of a soft dragging sound, or a heartbeat sound.

2. Weird sounds. These are good if they sound *like* something, but not like something exactly. Record the sound of soup bubbling—it sounds like hot lava or something worse. Fingernails scratching on blackboards are good. Dog howls and cat yowls slowed down and dog howls speeded up—both are good.

3. Chains to rattle and clank.

4. Crashes and blood-curdling screams. Use sparingly.

5. Crazy hysterical laughter.

Pick out sounds that go with the spooks in your spook house. Remember that loud noises aren't necessarily the scariest.

More suggestions.....

It's a good idea to have a little help. Let one person handle sound effects, another take money. Someone else will be needed to perform all the tricks that require people. Whoever takes the money could act as a guide to take the littlest kids through by the hand if they don't come with an older brother or sister.

Charge 5¢ or 10¢, not more. Don't let too many people into the spook house at once. It is better to have them line up outside rather than inside. And it's good advertising too.

If you know all the kids in your neighborhood, you and your spook house associates should dress up in scary outfits and take hand-written invitations around to each kid. To make it more mysterious, do it after dark. The invitations might say something like this.

EDDIE ALBERT
IS INVITED TO VISIT THE 13TH STREET
SCARY ****** SINISTER
SPOOK HOUSE!!!
OCTOBER 31 BETWEEN 2:00 AND 5:00
THIS INVITATION IS FROM THE
MONSTER, THE *VAMPIRE*,
AND *HERBIE HOROWITZ*
ADMISSION 5¢

76

The Gourd and Corn Folks

Here's how to turn 60¢ worth of seed that you plant in the spring into $25.00 worth of Thanksgiving decorations in the fall. For this business, Mother Nature is your partner. She turns seeds into beautiful ears of many-colored corn and wonderful lumpy, white, yellow, orange, and green gourds—a pretty amazing bit of work. All you have to do is help her out a little and, when she is through with the hard part, offer it all for sale. That's the easy part!

First, go to the nursery and find two seed packets. The ones you want are marked "Ornamental Corn" and "Gourds, Small Fruited Mixed," or similar words. Look at the pictures on the packets. The corn should be crazy colors and so should the gourds.

Read the instructions on the back of the seed pack and follow them carefully. Both gourds and corn like lots of sun. Be sure to plant them in good soil where there is sun most of the day. Ask at the nursery for advice if you're not sure how to plant the seeds.

Keep your garden soil moist. Both kinds of plants need water at their roots. If you plant early in May, they will be ready for picking about the time you go back to school. Be sure to harvest them before the first frost comes. Dry the corn and gourds in a warm, dry place. Hang the corn up high (where warm air circulates) in bunches. Spread the gourds out on a tray or table. Don't pile them up. If you want, varnish the gourds to make them shiny.

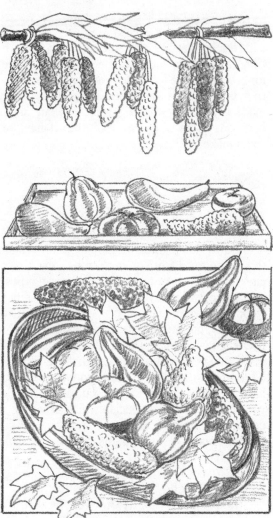

Around the first week in November, send out an announcement that you have Thanksgiving decorations for sale. You could sell the corn in bunches of three for 75¢, gourds for 25¢ or 50¢ each, depending on size. Or you could make up assortments with some colorful leaves to sell as table decorations. Charge $2.00 or more for assortments.

77

The Down-home Christmas Company

This idea is for kids who especially like Christmas. It's a good way to fill up your school vacation with things that are guaranteed to give you the Christmas spirit, and it will help you earn money for presents. The idea is for you and some of your friends to form a kid's company to bring handmade Christmas stuff to people in your neighborhood. Here are some of the things you could make.

Down-home green wreaths

The first thing to do is to gather some greens. There are lots of things that make good Christmas wreaths: any kind of pine (except maybe the very long-needle types), juniper, redwood, fir, holly. Even things like boxwood, eucalyptus, or bay can be used. If you live in the city, go to the first Christmas tree lot that opens in your neighborhood. Ask the manager if you can have the little branches that are trimmed off the trees. If you live in the country, you may have trees in your yard that you can trim. (Get your folks to help you decide which branches to cut.) Ask neighbors who have good trees if you can have some of their greens. Promise to make them a free wreath in return.

You Will Need
heavy wire (about the weight of a
coat hanger)
fine wire
wire snips
pruning shears
red weatherproof ribbon

First, make a frame to build your wreath on. Using the heavy wire, make two rings, one about 16 inches in diameter and one about 15 inches in diameter. Position them one inside the other and attach them at several points with the fine wire.

Cut the greens into short sprays. They should be no more than 7 inches long. Make neat bundles of greens with three or four sprays laid one on top of the other and wired together at the stems. Leave at least 5 inches of wire at the ends. Lay a bundle of greens on the frame and wire it firmly in place. Place the next bundle over the first, overlapping enough to cover the stems, and wire it into place. Continue to attach bundles, each overlapping the one before, until the entire frame is covered. Tuck the stems of the last bundle under the top of the first bundle to hide the wire. Tie a big, beautiful bow of ribbon, and wire it to the wreath.

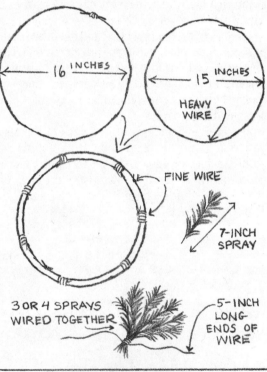

Make sure that your bundles are good and full and that they overlap enough to make a fine, fat wreath. If you have some pretty, little pinecones, you could wire on a few for added decoration. Sell these door-to-door for $5.00 to $8.00. (You could make two sizes.) Or take them back to the Christmas tree lot and ask if they'd like to buy the wreaths from you. Sell the wreaths for $3.50; the lot can sell them for $5.00.

Some other things to make with greens

Here are some more ideas of things you can make with the greens you've collected.

1. **Door swags.** If you have some boughs that are particularly beautiful just as they are, don't cut them up for wreaths. Wire two or three branches of different lengths and types together. Tie a large red bow and a cluster of pinecones over the wire and sell them for front-door decorations. You should be able to get $3.00 to $4.00 for a nice swag.

2. **Kissing balls.** Cut some sprays of greens: short-needle pine or boxwood is especially good for these. Make the sprays no more than 4 inches long. You can use a potato or a Styrofoam ball about the size of a hardball for the center. Stick greens into it to form a dense green ball. If the stems are too soft to poke in, wire toothpicks to them first. Wire a sprig of mistletoe to a toothpick and hang it from the bottom. Suspend the ball from a long, red ribbon. Sell the kissing balls for $3.00 each.

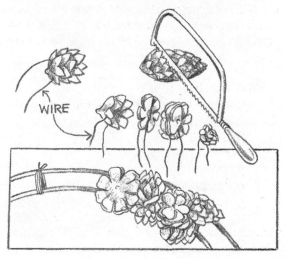

3. **Pinecone wreaths.** If you can find a good supply of different kinds of pinecones, you can make pretty wreaths using just pinecones. The small ones can be used as they are, but big ones look better when they are cut in half so they don't stick out too far. Saw them across with a coping saw. You can even slice the cones several times and use all of the slices. Wire the cones onto a wreath frame. Pack them together tightly so that the wires and frame don't show. You should be able to sell these for $8.00 to $10.00.

WIRE

The pinecone wreaths look especially nice when used on top of a rather flat green wreath. Don't put on a ribbon; that would be too much. Show your customers how they look together, and maybe you can sell *two* wreaths.

4. **Grapevine wreaths.** Grapevines for wreaths are easiest to work with if they are gathered when they are young and green, but you can gather them any time. You may be able to find wild grapevines in the woods, or you can ask for trimmings from your neighbors' vines. Try to cut vines about 6 to 7 feet long. Strip off all the leaves and leaf stems, but leave on the twisty tendrils. Bend one vine into an 18-inch circle, weaving it around and around itself to hold it together. Add another vine, twisting it around and around the circle and weaving it through the first vine. Keep adding vines, you may need five or six, until you have a good, solid wreath. Let your wreaths dry lying flat in a warm place. Make several sizes. Decorate them with red-and-green plaid or gingham ribbons. Sell them for $3.00, $4.00, or $5.00 depending on the size.

Note: Clematis vines will work exactly the same way as the grapevines.

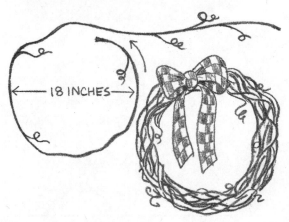

5. **Pasta snowflakes.** You've probably been cutting out paper snowflakes since you were five, but have you ever made spaghetti or manicotti or rigatoni snowflakes? A lot of people probably don't know about these wonderful ornaments. They're easy to make and look beautiful on the tree or suspended by threads in a mobile or just hanging in the window.

You will need some waxed paper, white glue, and a package of every different kind of pasta you can find at the grocery store. Get the little skinny ones like vermicelli and flat ones like fettuccine. There are seashell shapes and bowknots and circles and wagon wheels, thin noodles and fat noodles and bent ones and twisted ones. The more types you have to work with, the better your snowflakes will be.

Arrange the pieces of pasta in a snowflake design on a piece of waxed paper. When you get one that looks pretty, glue it together with small dabs of white glue. Make sure that you get glue every place one piece touches another. Let the snowflake dry thoroughly, and then gently peel off the waxed paper. Hang it with a loop of heavy-duty black sewing thread. Sell your pasta ornaments for 25¢ to $1.00, depending on the size.

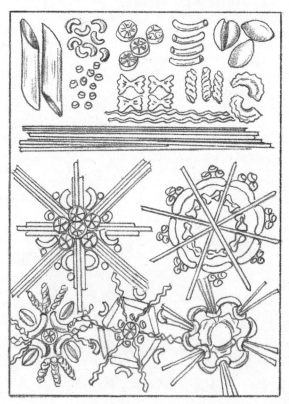

The Happy Holiday Giftwrap Service

Half the fun of getting and giving presents is the anticipation—on the one side, wondering what's in some mysterious-looking box or bundle, and on the other, knowing the secret but not telling. If the present is wrapped in some exotic way, to look like something it isn't, or like something it is, that makes it even more exciting. You can be part of the excitement by going into the gift-wrapping business.

If this idea appeals to you, you probably have all sorts of ideas already about ways to make presents look interesting. Since two noggins are better than one, I'll just throw in a few suggestions that you may not have thought of.

Prewrapped Boxes

Start collecting boxes of different sizes and shapes. It doesn't matter if they're a little grubby or have some sort of ugly advertising on them, but they shouldn't be crushed or lopsided. Look the boxes over and decide what sort of present might fit in each size or shape. Some are just right for clothes, like shirts or sweaters; others may be good for a doll or a pair of slippers. Some are very obvious, like tie boxes and jewelry boxes. Sort them by types, and then decide what kinds of people might get a present in that type of box. Make a list of them, just so you don't lose track and make too many for kids or for grown-ups or for boys or for girls. You should have a good selection.

Pick out a box and decide what might go in it. Then pick out the kind of paper you are going to use to wrap it. Look inside the box. If it looks used and a little dirty, pick out some paper for a new lining. Mend any broken corners with paper tape.

Reline the inside of the box if it looks grubby. Cover the outside of the lid and the bottom of the box. Use a thin paper and glue it down well around the edges so that the lid will not fit too tightly over the box.

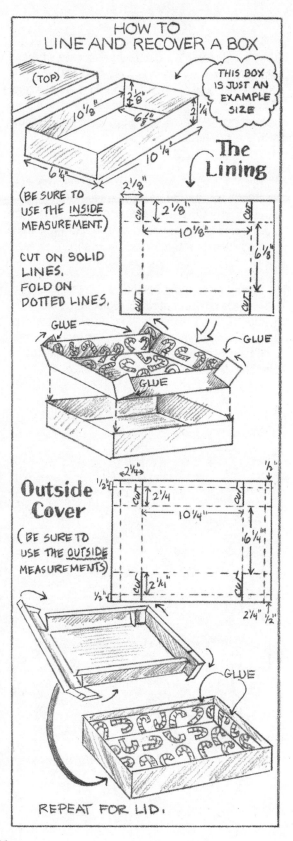

HOW TO LINE AND RECOVER A BOX

(TOP)

THIS BOX IS JUST AN EXAMPLE SIZE

The Lining

(BE SURE TO USE THE INSIDE MEASUREMENT.)

CUT ON SOLID LINES. FOLD ON DOTTED LINES.

GLUE

Outside Cover

(BE SURE TO USE THE OUTSIDE MEASUREMENTS)

GLUE

REPEAT FOR LID.

Plain-colored, prewrapped boxes look nice if they are decorated. You might decorate a tie box with small cutouts of ties. Use wild patterns and colors that no one would be caught dead wearing. Tie it with (you guessed it) an old tie! You'll have to shorten it, so cut out the middle and sew the two ends together.

Jewelry boxes should be glamorous. Try covering a box with foil paper and glue one of those small bristly Christmas trees to the center of the lid. Decorate the tree with shiny beads or sequins and sprinkle it with silver or gold glitter.

For a box that is to hold a doll, cut pictures of all sorts of dolls out of catalogs and magazines and paste them all over the box, upside down and sideways and every which way, or make a paper doll-baby that fits into a little bunting pasted to the box. The baby could be a gift card.

For patchwork boxes, cut patchwork patterns out of pieces of construction paper of different colors or of wrapping paper with small prints. Patchwork looks best on square boxes. Tie them with gingham ribbons.

To make silhouette boxes, lay a pretty spray of pine or holly on a plain-colored box. Carefully and very briefly spray directly down on the branch with a spray enamel of contrasting color. It will make a lovely shadow print of the branch. Experiment on paper a few times before you try it on a box. You can use this same technique to spray around grasses or flowers or cutout paper snowflakes, anything that has a pleasing outline.

Perhaps you would like to create some origami boxes. Make a scene on the top of a box using origami animals, flowers, or birds pasted against an appropriate background.

Some things just won't fit into boxes or for one reason or another just seem to go better in a bag. So at the same time you are collecting boxes, start looking for and saving bags. You can use all sizes. Ask a friendly grocery clerk for some fresh, unused brown paper bags. Get the plain ones with no advertising on them. Some grocery stores have plain white ones too. Usually they'll give you a bunch of them. Pick up any plain plastic bags that you see, even the ones with handles. They can be clear or opaque, but try to find the ones that don't have any writing on them. Always save the plastic net bags that hams and fruit and onions sometimes come in.

Brown paper bags can be used in a number of ways. They can be folded over at the top, with slits cut for ribbon to be threaded through. Tie the ribbon in a nice bow with long streamers. Tuck sprigs of pine and holly under the bow.

You can print all over the bags with some sort of motif, using a potato stamp (see The Hand-and-Foot Printer) or a stencil. Cut a pattern out

of light cardboard and spray with bright-colored enamel spray paint. This looks especially good on clear plastic bags because you can see the design from both sides.

The plastic net bags look neat if they are used over an opaque plastic bag and then tied with ribbon. Cut the handles off the plastic shopping bags and trim the top even or in a zigzag pattern. If your mom has pinking shears, ask her if you can use them to make an edging.

Start collecting wrapping paper long before the Christmas season. In fact, a good time to find wrapping paper is right after Christmas when many stores put it on sale. Don't overlook some papers that may seem pretty commonplace, but that will make interesting wrapping paper. Newspapers in a foreign language, particularly ones that use a different alphabet, such as Chinese or Arabic or Greek, make nifty-looking packages. Use the sheets with the fewest pictures. Make up a sample using the newspaper stock-market quotations and tie it with black or bright red ribbon.

Potato prints can be used on a lot of different kinds of paper to create interesting effects. They look great on the kind of rice paper that has threads running through it. The same print on tissue paper will look completely different, and on shelf paper will look like something else again.

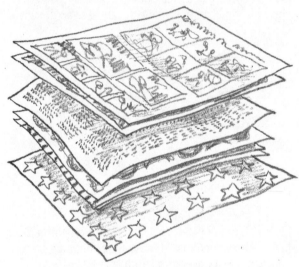

How to Sell Your Wrapping Service

Make up some samples of wrapped gifts. Have a good supply of prewrapped boxes and a large selection of wrapping paper, bags, and ribbons ready before you try to sell your service. Load some of your choicest samples into a wagon or a basket and go door-to-door around your neighborhood. Offer to bring supplies to people's houses and wrap their presents.

Many organizations have Christmas bazaars where you could set up a booth. Have a poster and a price list to display. Hand out flyers with your telephone number.

HAPPY HOLIDAY GIFTWRAP SERVICE
SARAH COOK, PROPRIETOR   556-4437

PREWRAPPED BOXES
   small .... 50¢
   medium .... 75¢
   large $1.00

RICE PAPER
   full sheet .... 50¢
   half sheet .... 25¢

TISSUE PAPER
   full sheet/lining .... 30¢
   half sheet/lining .... 15¢

SHELF PAPER
   by the yard .... 50¢

WIDE RIBBON
   by the yard .... 50¢

NARROW RIBBON
   by the yard .... 30¢

PRICES INCLUDE LABOR
ESTIMATES GIVEN FOR CUSTOM WORK

The
Wax and Wick
Works

Inge and Berit Larsen live in San Francisco. During the year, whenever they get the spirit (and always at Christmas!), they make candles— usually with the help of their big sister, Lael. Because these girls have wonderful ideas for what looks nice, they make beautiful candles. Here is how they do it:

You Will Need
    candle-making wax from the craft store
    Parawax from the grocery store (pretty expensive!)
      or broken candles and stubs from your neighbors (free)
    squares of colored wax, or crayons (to color clear wax)
    sticks for stirring
    wicks
    scissors
    several 1-pound coffee cans
    a spoon (to test the color of the wax)
    an old saucepan
    an old pie pan
    a large old bowl
    an eggbeater
    paper milk cartons
    frozen juice containers
    commercial candle molds (if you want to buy them)
    eggs
    sand
    newspapers (lots)

Making the candles. Melt a chunk of wax in a 1-pound coffee can set in a saucepan of water. Never try to melt wax directly over the burner. Wax is very flammable (catches fire easily), so handle it carefully. Add crayons or colored wax to get the color you want. You can prepare several colors at the same time (in separate cans).

Dipped candles. Fill a large bowl with cold water. Dip a length of wick into a can of melted wax, then quickly into the bowl of water. Straighten the wick. Repeat this process, alternately dipping the wick in wax and then in water, until your candle is nice and plump and pretty.

Rainbow candles. Pour a little bit of colored wax into a frozen-juice container. Wrap a piece of wick around a pencil. Place the pencil across the top of the container so the wick will hang directly in the middle. As soon as the first color hardens, pour in the next color. Keep adding colors until the container is full. When the final color is hard, peel off the container.

Squishy candles. Fill a big bowl or pan with cold water. Pour melted wax into the water. Shape a squishy candle with your hands, inserting the wick as you squish.

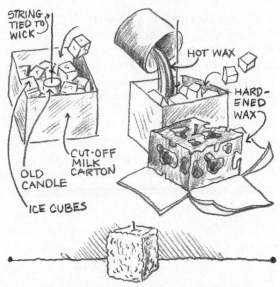

Roll-ups. Pour a thin layer of wax into an old pie pan or a flat cake pan. When the wax is solid enough so that you can lift it, lay a wick across one edge and slowly roll the wax and wick into the shape of a tube. (If the wax sticks to the pan, try coating the pan with cooking oil or Mold Release, a special "stick preventer" you can buy at craft stores.) Shape the candle with your hands. Flatten the bottom so the candle will stand up.

Frosted candles. Buy a couple of boxes of Parawax at the grocery store. Melt two of the rectangular pieces. Stick four pieces together with melted Parawax, with a wick running up the center. Take the melted wax off the burner and beat it with an eggbeater until it forms a froth. Frost the outside of the candle with frothy wax. You will have to work quickly to finish before the froth hardens too much.

Ice-cube candles. Cut a paper milk carton in half, or use a pint-size container. Put an old candle in the center of the carton and hold it upright with a string tied to the wick. Place some ice cubes around the candle and quickly pour in some colored wax. Wait until the wax has hardened; then pour off the water from the melted ice. Add a few more ice cubes and repeat the process until the container is full. When the wax has hardened, strip off the container. Surprise! Your candle has holes.

Egg candles. Prick a small hole in the big end of an egg with a darning needle. Make a larger hole, about the size of a dime, in the small end. Empty out the contents by blowing through the small hole. Wash the egg in warm soapy water and let it dry. Tie a knot in the end of a wick and thread it from the outside through the small hole. Hold the eggshell upright in an egg carton with the wick stretched tight up the center and fill it with melted wax. Let the wax harden and peel away the eggshell.

Sand-cast candles. Fill a large bowl or box with fine sand. Dampen the sand until it sticks together. Make some fancy-shaped hole in the sand with your hands or by pressing something into it. Suspend a wick down the center. Or you can put in several wicks. Pour in the melted wax. Wait several hours for it to harden. When you're sure it's hard, dig out the candles and see what you've made. If the wax is very hot when you pour it into the sand mold, you will end up with a thick crust of sand on the outside. If it is cooler, only a little sand will stick to it.

Finished candles. Inge and Berit took their candles to the neighborhood flea market and made $25.00. They made most of the money from candles, but they also sold old jewelry, buttons, Cracker Jack toys, comic books, and other valuable junk that they had found when they cleaned their rooms the day before. Grown-ups bought the candles, and kids bought the junk.

JIMMIE'S FLOATING CHRISTMAS CANDLES

A thrifty boy used to make floating candles from candle ends and crayons every Christmastime. He poured the melted wax into Jell-O molds and muffin tins. The candles always looked beautiful floating with flowers or greens in a big bowl on the dining room table. He charged 25¢ each and sold them door-to-door a few days before Christmas.

This is a good way to start in the candle business because you don't have to buy any supplies. You can reuse the wicks from the candle stubs.

First, grease the molds.

The Hot-Mulled-Cider Stand

This is a wintertime version of the old-fashioned lemonade stand. It's not hard to figure out where you should go to find customers. Go anyplace where lots of people are out having fun in the snow. Set up business at the local skating pond or a favorite sledding hill. It's best to have a partner in this business. It will get pretty cold just standing around selling cider, so have a friend to spell you. Take turns sledding or skating and selling.

WARM-AND-COSY MULLED CIDER
- **1 gallon apple cider**
- **4 sticks of cinnamon (don't use ground cinnamon)**
- **2 tsp. ground nutmeg**
- **2 tsp. whole cloves**

Put all the ingredients in a big pot and heat it until it's just about to boil. Remove from the burner and fill preheated thermos bottles, distributing the cinnamon sticks and cloves proportionately.

Wrap the thermos bottles in thick rolls of newspaper and pack them in a box. Load them on a sled and head for the scene of action.

Serve your cider in small Styrofoam cups. You can figure out how much to charge by dividing the price of the cider by the number of servings in a gallon. Then add the price of the spices (the cinnamon will be the most expensive) and the cups, and some profit for you.

The Anytime-It-Snows Shovelers Company

When winter comes, there probably isn't anything you like so much as the first snow. And there probably isn't anything you like less than shoveling it off the front walk, right?

Shoveling snow is hard work, and when you don't feel like doing it, it's no fun. But here is a way to set up a business that will make the job a little more fun and earn you money besides.

Collect three friends who are willing to be your partners. Everyone has to understand that the Shovelers Company has to be dependable. Which means when it snows, all the partners have to be ready to work, no matter what.

Then make up some handouts. Take them around the neighborhood, and post them on bulletin boards wherever you can. They should say something like this.

Whoever's phone number is on the handout is the dispatcher. The dispatcher calls each member until he or she finds someone who can do the work. (Sometimes you just can't, and it isn't because you're lazy.) The dispatcher should distribute the jobs fairly, so everyone has a chance to work. In heavy snows, it will be more fun and easier to work in teams.

The most important thing about this business is that you must work right away when it snows because people will depend on you. It may even mean getting up early so that the woman down the street can get her car out to go to work at 8:00 A.M.

If you have good friends you can count on, you'll have a great winter business. Charge at least $1.00 for short walks, more for longer ones and driveways.

When it SNOWS, DON'T GET STUCK !!
Call this number and we will come to SHOVEL your WALK or DRIVEWAY.
★ We bring our own tools.
★ Your satisfaction guaranteed.
CALL ANYTIME AFTER SCHOOL OR ON WEEKENDS.
★ 675-1104 ASK FOR JIM

I'll be indoors with the hot chocolate.

Draft Stoppers

When cold winter winds start to blow and people start to think about ways to keep their houses warm, that's the time to go into the insulation business. If you think that insulation sounds dull, that's because you don't know about draft stoppers.

Draft stoppers are crazy little critters who spend their time lying in front of leaky window frames and badly fitted doors just to keep the rest of us warm and cozy. Draft stoppers are fun to design and make. You should be able to sell quite a few to shivering friends and neighbors.

To do a good job, at least part of the draft stopper must be the right shape to cover the crack under a door or window. That means about 36 or more inches long and about 3 inches in diameter. The easiest to make are silly serpents with big googly eyes and loppity tongues. Make the serpents out of bright-colored fabrics, stripes, or prints.

Cut a piece of fabric about 42 inches long and 8 inches wide. Fold it in half, right sides together, and sew it the down the long side to make a long tube. Sew one end closed, tapering it slightly (the tail). Turn it right side out and stuff it with cotton batting. Turn under a small hem on the open end. Cut a long forked tongue out of red felt. Sew the open end together, gathering it slightly where the tongue sticks out. Make the eyes out of big buttons, or cut them out of black and white felt and sew them on.

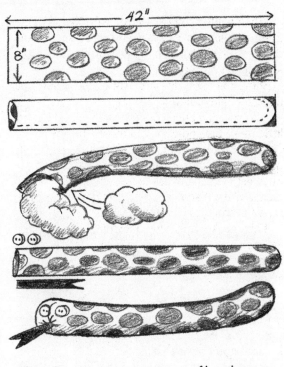

A cat or a raccoon or any sort of imaginary animal with a long tail would make a good draft stopper. And you don't have to make animals. I've made some that look like flowers that are lying down: the stems are the working part. You will probably think of all sorts of new and different ideas once you start making and selling these handy little items.

See "Thread and Needleworks" for ways to sell these.

91

Thread and Needleworks

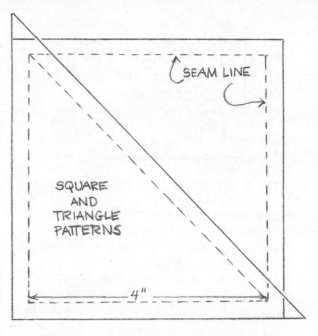

SEAM LINE

SQUARE
AND
TRIANGLE
PATTERNS

4"

This is an idea that's good anytime. It's something to do when there's nothing to do, when it's raining outside for example, or when you're getting over the flu and feel fine but can't go out for two days. Or when you're just plain bored. All you need is an old-time all-around jumble-dump ragbag. You know. That big bag of scraps that your mom has in the closet that she never uses but won't throw away.

Well, tell her that it's really a natural resource in disguise and that you're going to make a miracle out of it. (No one can resist a miracle.) Then get a needle and thread and try making one of these surefire scrap recipes.

Patchwork pillows. These are fun to make because you can use some of the pretty, old-fashioned patchwork patterns, and you don't have to make the same one twice. Each side of your pillow can be a different design. Get some books from the library that show patterns. Pick out several that you like and trace them. Stick to the simple, straight-line designs at first, until you get to be an expert patcher. Here are two patterns that are good for beginners.

1. Draw the patterns on tracing paper and cut them out. Do it carefully, making sure that all the corners are exactly square. You will need only the one square patch pattern for Nine-patch and the square and the triangular patterns for Shoofly.

2. Iron the fabric flat, and then cut out enough patches of each color. Cut them very carefully along the grain of the fabric.

3. If you are making Nine-patch, sew the squares together in three strips of three patches each, alternating colors. Iron each strip so it's flat, and then sew the strips together and iron them again.

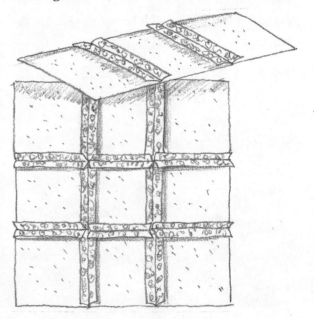

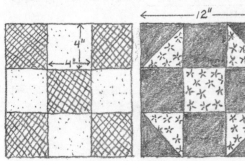

12"

4"

4"

12"

4. If you are making Shoofly, first sew the triangular patches together to form squares and iron them, and then assemble the patchwork as you did in the Nine-patch.

5. With the right sides together, sew the front and back of the pillow cover together, leaving one side open for stuffing. You can make both sides of your pillow in patchwork, or you can have one side plain.

6. Stuff the pillow with shredded foam rubber or polyester and sew up the opening.

Shooting-star beanbags.. These are fun to make and play with and just a little different from the usual beanbags.

1. Draw the star-shaped pattern and cut it out.

SEAM LINE

CUT TWO

2. Cut two stars out of some pretty, starry fabric and sew them together along the seam lines, right sides together. Leave a small section between points open for filling.

LEAVE OPEN

3. Turn the star right side out and press flat.

4. Make a tail out of strands of yarn in pretty colors, or you can use narrow Mylar ribbon to make a glittery tail. Tie a knot at one end to hold them together.

5. Fill the star with dried beans, rice, or lentils. Insert the knotted end of the tail and sew up the opening.

93

Pincushion flowers. These pincushions are fun to make because they don't take long and because you can use up all those funny little bits of silky material that are too pretty to throw away and too little to use for anything else.

1. Draw the petal patterns and cut them out.

2. Cut out a circle of fabric 7 inches in diameter for the center cushion.

3. Run a line of hand stitching about ½ inch from the edge of the circle. Use a double thread so that it will be good and strong. You don't have to make very small stitches.

4. Stuff the circle with polyester and pull the thread tight to form a firm ball. Sew it closed.

5. For the rose, make five large petals and five small petals by sewing the fronts and backs together along the seam lines, right sides facing.

6. Turn them right side out and iron flat.

7. Gather the petals along the open end with three or four stitches.

8. Sew the petals to the bottom of the cushion, small petals first, then the large petals.

9. To finish the bottom, cut a 2-inch circle of cardboard and a 3-inch circle of fabric.

10. Cover the cardboard circle as shown.

11. Sew it with small, neat stitches over the place where the petals are attached.

12. Stick about ten yellow round-headed pins in the center of the cushion to look like stamens.

The rose will be especially pretty if you use three shades of pink, the deepest pink for the center. The daisy has a yellow center and white petals. You can think of some other flowers that will make good pincushions, or use your imagination and design some fantastic blossoms.

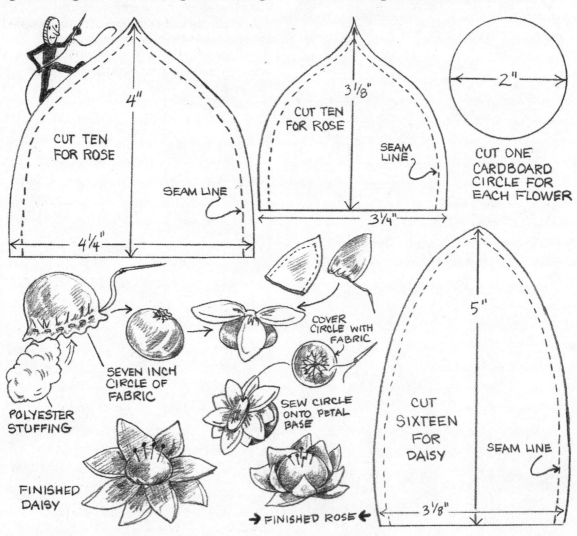

94

Kewpie hats. You can make one of these funny little hats out of a piece of fabric 20 inches square. It will fit anyone and look good on either kids or grown-ups, depending on how you decorate it.

1. Cut a circle of fabric 20 inches in diameter.

2. Fold it in half, right sides together, and sew it together around the curved edge. Leave about 4 inches open for turning.

3. Turn it right side out and press it flat.

4. Sew up the opening.

5. Fold it into a cone shape and sew up the back with small, neat stitches.

6. Decorate it with ribbons or flowers or tassels or anything you want.

Washable baby balls. These are easy to make and are a good way to use up small fabric scraps. Since these balls are for little babies, they should be made of washable cotton material. Small patterns or checked ginghams look best.

Here are directions for making a soft baseball.

1. Cut two pieces of contrasting fabric the shape of the pattern.

2. Sew them together as shown, leaving about 3 inches open for stuffing. These balls are easier to sew by hand as you have to keep adjusting the fabric to make it fit.

3. Stuff the ball with polyester or shredded foam rubber and sew up the opening.

4. Topstitch the way a baseball is, with a bright-colored embroidery yarn.

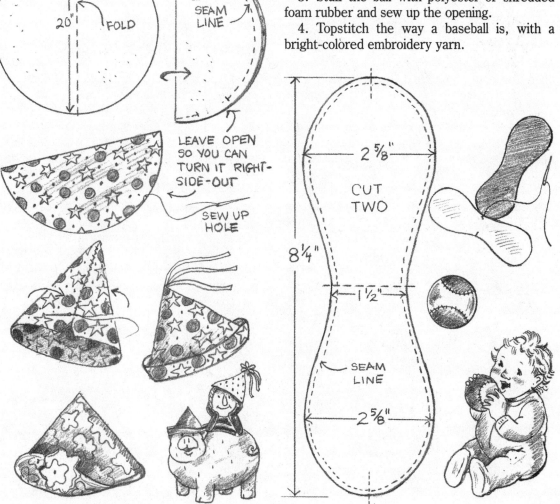

Or you could make a soft melon ball. Here's how to do it.

1. Cut six melon-slice sections from various fabric scraps.
2. Sew them together along the seam lines, leaving one side open for stuffing.
3. Stuff the melon ball and sew up the opening.

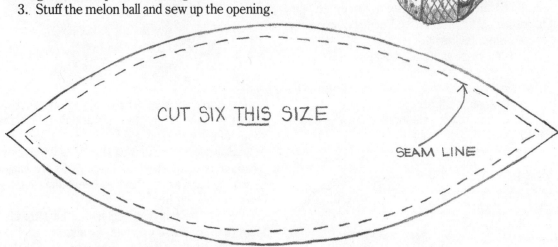

CUT SIX THIS SIZE

SEAM LINE

Once you've made a couple of these items and you like what you've made, get some friends to help you make more. Do it on a Saturday morning or a vacation day. Get everyone around a big table and divide up the work. If you all have a good time and want to do it again, you've got yourself a Thread and Needleworks. Keep track of what each person makes so you can pay people when you sell the work. You could keep a Needleworks Book, with a page for each person. That way your friends can work any time they have a chance. You all enter a record of what you make on your own page. A page might look like this:

GREG

DATE	WORK
2/6	2 pillows - cut out
2/9	1 pillow stitched and stuffed
2/14	1 pillow stitched and stuffed
2/18	4 stars cut out, 2 stitched
2/23	2 stars stitched, 4 stuffed

When you have made a few of each item, take them around to some stores. Good places to try are gift shops, toy stores, book shops, children's clothing stores, and so on. Make a little tag for each item, saying that it was made by the kids of the Thread and Needleworks.

Ask the store owner how much you should charge for each item. If you think the price sounds right, and if the store owner is willing, leave your work there "on consignment." That means the store sells your items and pays you afterward. The store keeps some of the money in exchange for selling your work. Record in your Needleworks Book who took what items on consignment and the date. Once a month, check back with the store owners to see what has been sold and collect any money that they owe you.

I'll bet right this minute there are five toys lying around your house that you got a long time ago and don't ever play with anymore and wouldn't mind giving away. If everyone you know has five toys like that, how many toys does that make?

You can start a toy hospital now and fix up old toys slick as a whistle and sell all you can fix. There are good reasons for that. First, most used toys can be fixed up easily and look almost as good as new. Second, what is an old toy to you will be new to someone else. Third, there are lots of grown-ups who are tired of buying new toys that aren't very good for big prices. Those people will be your best customers, and there are a lot of them.

If that hasn't convinced you, here are some examples of ways you can make old toys like new again. Once you start, you'll get lots of ideas of your own.

Rag Dolls

Sew up ripped seams and patch holes. Use interesting patches, like heart shapes or butterflies. If you use felt for the patches, they're easy to cut out and sew on. Add new yarn hair. Brighten the mouth and cheeks with felt markers. You could sew on buttons for eyes or get some of the goofy moving eyes that are sold at craft stores. Make a simple dress. Tie a ribbon for her dress and one for her hair.

Plastic Dolls

Wash the doll well with soap and water. Use a little cleanser if it's really grubby. Arms and legs will usually just snap back into place. Comb her hair and curl it by twisting it around a pencil and spraying it with hair spray. Wash and iron her clothes or make new ones.

Assorted Blocks

Collect a lot of wooden blocks. Sand any rough edges and paint them bright colors, using lead-free enamel paint. Find a good sturdy box that they'll fit into neatly. Paint it or cover it with wrapping paper.

Stuffed Animals

Replace any lost stuffing with cotton batting and sew up the seams. If there are parts missing, make new ones. You won't be able to make them match the animal, so make them funny instead. Eyes and mouths can be cut out of felt and sewn or glued on. If you are good at it, embroider them. Don't use buttons on toys for babies because they can come off and little kids may swallow them.

Metal Toys

Metal cars and trucks may need a new coat of paint. If they are chipped and rusty, sand them very well before you repaint them. If you are using a spray paint, cover all the trim, the tires, and windows with masking tape before you start. After the paint is dry, do the details with a small brush. Model paints are good for this job.

How to get toys. Start with your friends. Tell them your idea and ask them to help by giving you their old toys. (You could also arrange to pay them 10¢ for each one when you sell it.) Ask your PTA to put a notice in the school newsletter, or put up a notice at church or on the supermarket bulletin board.

Where to do the fixing. Pick a place, such as a basement or garage, where you can use paint and tools and make kind of a mess without getting in the way. An old, fixed-up chicken coop or garden shed would be perfect.

When you get the toys, sort them into types. See if you can put two incomplete toys together to make one whole one.

Put the toys on shelves or in boxes until you can get to work on them. If they are in a place where you can look at them, you'll get ideas for how to fix them up while you work on something else.

Selling what you fix. Don't offer your new/old toys for sale until you have fixed a good-size batch. Fix at least two or three dozen. Decide in advance how much you should charge. Try to keep the prices much lower than the prices for new toys.

When the toys are ready, you could take them to a flea market or you could have a big toy sale. Distribute flyers around the neighborhood and have a large sign in the front yard.

FOR SALE HERE
TOYS REMADE BY KIDS
IN OUR
TOYS FIXIT FACTORY

After Christmas is over, when the ground is still covered with snow, and it seems like winter is going to go on forever, people start to hang around indoors and complain about the weather and vegetate in front of the TV. This is a great time to get out there and stir things up. Put on a Winter Carnival.

Talk about it with your family and friends and neighbors. Try to get the adults interested; they're probably feeling just as dull and restless as you are. When everyone is enthusiastic and raring to go, decide where to have the festival. You might want to spread out over three or four people's front yards. If there's still plenty of snow piled around, start things off with a snow-sculpture contest. Charge a small fee (10¢ for kids, 25¢ for adults) for people who want to enter the contest. Collect the fee ahead of time and use the money to buy prizes. Assign each entrant a spot where he or she can build a work of art. It will work best if you can get some grown-up with a snowplow attachment on a lawn tractor to make snow piles at each location.

Have prizes and fancy certificates for best adult sculpture, best kid sculpture, ugliest, funniest, most original, biggest, smallest, and so on. Once neighbors have come out of their houses to see or participate in the snow-sculpture event, they'll be ready to enjoy themselves at the rest of the carnival.

Some more ideas. Here are more ideas for the Winter Carnival.

1. Have a booth selling hot, mulled cider and carrot cake.

2. Pile up snow for a little kids' flying-saucer run. Charge 5¢ for five turns. Use big bowls and trays for flying saucers.

3. Have a booth where you sell all the nifty things you've been making all winter, like candles, pincushions, beanbags, and pillows.

4. Peddle hot, roasted chestnuts.

5. Dress up like horses. Charge little kids 10¢ for an exciting snorting, galloping sleigh ride around the carnival grounds.

6. Set up a King-of-the-Glacier game. Build a low mound of snow with a flat top big enough for two people to stand face-to-face at arm's length. On the night before the carnival, wet down the top so it freezes. The object of the game is for two people to stand on top of the mound, with one hand behind their backs, trying to push each other off the mound without falling off themselves. Charge 10¢ per game.

7. Run a Knock-the-Head-off-the-Snowman game. Build a good solid snowman, small size. Make up a whole bunch of head-size snowballs (about the size of a grapefruit) and have them in reserve. Mark off a good throwing range. (You could have one for older kids and adults and a shorter one for little kids.) Charge 10¢ for three snowball throws to try to knock the head off the snowman. The head should be sitting loose so that a good hard hit will topple it. Prizes could be a free turn on the King-of-the-Glacier game. (You'd have to run the two games in partnership and share the profits.)

8. Have a sugaring-off candy booth. Boil maple syrup (or any commercial pancake syrup) until it reaches the soft-ball stage (234 degrees). Dribble the hot syrup into a big pan of clean snow, a tablespoonful at a time. It will harden into delicious cold, chewy ribbons of candy. Keep the syrup warm on a camping stove and pour it right before your customers' eyes. Sell the lovely, gooey blobs for 10¢ each.

SUMMERTIMERS

Private Eye House Watchers

It may be vacation time for people, but cats and fish and white mice still need to be fed, and houseplants and gardens still need to be watered. Papers and mail should be collected and put somewhere out of sight. And if people don't use a timer, lights should be turned on and off so the bad guys don't spot an empty house. Be a vacation house watcher and earn your own vacation money.

SNIFF

To get started in the house-watching business, talk to neighbors who already know you. Tell them what you are prepared to do. If they are interested in having you house watch, sit down with them and make a list of all the things they want you to take care of. Work out a schedule for watering and pet feeding. You should start to keep a calendar, one with big spaces where you can write things down under each day. When you have several customers lined up, assign each one a color. Mark on your calendar in colored pen the days that each family will be away and list the things that you need to do for them. *This is important.* You don't want your customers to come home to a bowlful of dead goldfish or an AWOL mouser because you forgot to feed them. If you have to go into the house, put a great big, colored tag on the keys—one that's hard to miss and hard to lose. But don't write the owner's name or address on it. That way, you'll know who the keys belong to but nobody else will.

AUGUST   ○ = Smiths ◉ = Moores
● = O'Hares

SUN	MON	TUES	WED	THURS	FRI	SAT
		1	2	3	4	5
6	7	8	9	10	11	12
13	14	15	16	17	18	19
20	22	23	24	25	26	
	29	30	31			

15 *– DAILY
◉ – FEED CAT
   – WATER FRONT
✳ MAIL, PAPER
○ – WATER
✳ FEED FISH

101

Get a list of emergency phone numbers for each customer, a friend or relative you could call if there's a problem with the house. Have the name and number for their vet if you're caring for animals. And, of course, you should know the local emergency number for the police and fire department.

After you have house watched for people you know and have done a good job, they will probably recommend you to their friends. Remember, this is a job that you have to do every day without fail. Don't agree to do it unless you're sure you can stick to it.

What to charge. This is something that you will have to work out with your customers. It will depend on what you are supposed to do each day and how long it will take you. You could charge by the hour and mark down your time on the calendar. Or you might want to charge your customers a flat fee for the time they are gone. In either case, have a clear understanding of the arrangement beforehand.

BRET'S VISITING ZOOKEEPER BUSINESS

Bret has all sorts of jobs. He mows lawns and chops firewood and trims hedges, but his favorite job is being a visiting zookeeper. His biggest job was taking care of a whole bunch of animals for an entire month. There was a dog that he fed twice a day. He didn't have to take him for walks because there was a long run, but he did spend time playing with him because dogs need companionship almost more than they need food. Once a day he fed three chickens, two guinea pigs, and five fish—they were more interested in the food than in his company.

Old-Fashioned Lemonade

If it's hot outside and lemons aren't too expensive, maybe this is the day to think about setting up an old-time lemonade stand. If you live in a place where lots of people go by and can easily stop, then you can think about their coming to you. If you don't live in such a place, you had better think about taking your lemonade to them, wherever they are. But first, you have to think about the lemonade.

People like lemonade because it tastes good on a hot day: not too sweet, but cold, very wet, and good for a dry mouth. Your first job is to make the best lemonade anyone ever tasted. And here is the recipe.

Each batch should make 30 7-ounce cups. If you have paid 25¢ for each lemon, you'll have to sell each cup of lemonade for 25¢. If lemons are cheap, you could sell the lemonade for 10¢. Here is the arithmetic.

```
MONEY YOU SPEND:
  12 lemons ———————— $3.00
  2 cups sugar ————       .30
  30 paper cups ————       .90
              total ——— $4.20

MONEY YOU CHARGE:
  Sell 30 cups for
  25¢ each ————————— $7.50
  LESS TOTAL COST:    — 4.20

MONEY YOU MAKE — $3.30
```

On a hot day, in the right location, you might be able to sell two or three batches in one afternoon.

The Best LEMONADE Anyone Ever Tasted

THE VERY BEST LEMONADE IS MADE FROM FRESH LEMONS, SUGAR AND PURE, FRESH WATER. IF LEMONS ARE TOO EXPENSIVE (DON'T PAY MORE THAN 25¢ EACH), YOU HAD BETTER USE FROZEN LEMON JUICE, WHICH MAKES A PASSABLE, BUT NOT GREAT, LEMONADE.

1. MIX THE JUICE FROM A DOZEN BIG LEMONS WITH TWO CUPS OF SUGAR.

2. PUT THE MIXTURE IN A JAR WITH A LID AND SHAKE IT UP UNTIL THE SUGAR DISSOLVES.

3. IF YOU WANT TO MAKE PINK LEMONADE, ADD A FEW DROPS OF RED FOOD COLORING TO THE MIXTURE.

4. NEXT ADD 12 CUPS OF COLD WATER AND STIR IT WELL.

5. PUT THE MIXTURE IN A BIG THERMOS. FILL ANOTHER BIG THERMOS, THE WIDEMOUTHED KIND, WITH ICE CUBES. TO SERVE, PUT TWO ICE CUBES IN A 7-OUNCE PAPER CUP (USE TONGS). FILL THE CUP WITH LEMONADE. IF YOU USE MORE ICE IT WILL DILUTE THE LEMONADE.

Make a big sign. If you want people to stop their cars, it will help to make a sign that gives them time to stop. Ask the neighbors if you can put up signs on the way to your stand.

What is the right location? If you live in a place where people pass by *and can see your stand* in plenty of time to stop and pull over, you could try a street-side stand. But people who are walking or riding a bike are much more apt to stop. So try one along a bike path or downtown where there are shops. Here are two kinds of stands. Take your pick, or design one of your own. The most important thing (aside from the lemonade) is that you are *very visible*.

A ROLLING LEMONADE-WAGON-STAND

There are some tricks to the lemonade trade. Have some thin slices of lemon rind floating in it. That looks nice, smells good, and adds to the flavor. Also, you could charge 25¢ for the first glass and 15¢ for the second (especially if lemons are not expensive). You could sell homemade chocolate chip cookies for 15¢ each to go with the lemonade.

Remember! Making fresh, homemade lemonade is something that very few people take the time to do any more. Everyone is in such a hurry. You are probably the only place for miles around where a hot, thirsty traveler can get a refreshing drink of pure, cold lemonade.

A SIDEWALK STAND

America Needs Clean Dogs

Summer is the perfect time to start your own dog-wash service. Just think how many dogs you could wash if you and four of your friends set up a super-duper dog-wash production line in your backyard. Just think how many clean dogs and happy owners there would be.

This is how you might set up the jobs.

1. Manager/dog handler
2. Washer
3. Rinser
4. Dryer
5. Goodie giver

You Will Need
leashes (or rope)
two large, shallow, plastic or metal tubs
a hose and lots of water
dog shampoo or a mild soap
clean, old towels or rags
dog biscuits (for rewards)

How to advertise

Make some eye-catching posters with time, date, and price. Hang them in the local vet's office, pet store, and laundromat. Also, you could go around and tell your neighbors about your service. You might even get some appointments in advance. Charge $2.00 per wash. You could make this into a regular service, once every other week, if you have lots of dogs in your neighborhood. You might be able to wash ten dogs in one afternoon. Be sure to wear old clothes or your bathing suit.

105

The Yard People

A yard person is someone who makes money by taking care of yards—backyards, front yards, patios, or window boxes and mostly in the summertime. Yard people do things such as mowing lawns, or watering, or pulling weeds, or trimming hedges or shrubs. Sometimes yard people pick fruit, and sometimes they build or mend fences or paint lawn furniture. Mostly they do whatever their customers need to have done.

Summertime isn't the only time that yard people can find work. In fact, if you're thinking about going into business, spring is the time to start advertising. Make a flyer to distribute around your neighborhood. Offer to do some of the things that people usually start thinking about at that time of year.

When summer comes and you have more time, you might want some more business. Write another flyer to remind people about your service. Tell them you'll take care of their gardens while they're on vacation. Offer to weed, trim hedges, mow the grass, and water if there's a dry spell. You could pick vegetables and deliver them wherever the customer wants.

In the fall, too, there are chores that you can do. You can take down the screens you put up in the spring, put away the lawn furniture, rake leaves, and generally put the garden to bed for the winter.

What to charge. How much you charge really depends on what chores you are able to do. If you are doing some of the hard things, such as digging and carrying heavy screens and furniture, you can charge more. For light work, such as watering and weeding, charge less. You can charge by the job or by the hour. It's probably easiest to figure out a fair wage if you are paid by the hour, but you have to keep a careful account and *really work* the entire time you charge for.

A YARD GIRL

Renee Barnett is nine years old. She has gone into the watering business. She lives in California, where it doesn't rain all summer, so watering plants is a big job. She waters the plants in front of her neighbor's house four times a week. She keeps a record of the time she spends watering that looks something like this.

Mon.	In	4:26
	Out	4:35
Wed.	In	7:04
	Out	7:33
Thurs.	In	5:15
	Out	5:45
Sat.	In	2:08
	Out	3:20

Renee is hoping to get a dog-walking job too. That's what sounds like the most fun to her. She's saving her money to buy something really special.

Renee charges 50¢ for each half hour of watering. She can decide when she wants to do it, so it's an easy job to fit into her schedule.

This isn't the only job that Renee has. She is working for another neighbor, who wanted some stickers put on a brochure that he uses in his business. She got her jobs by putting flyers around her neighborhood. Renee's flyer said:

JOB WANTED - CAN DO ANYTHING
Walk your dog - I'm a dog expert.
Tutor your child - age six or seven preferred.
Water your plants - I talk to them, too.
FOR INFORMATION CALL
RENEE BARNETT - 472-4215

Beach Sitters

Do you love to spend the summer on the beach, but you'd still like to earn some spending money? Why not become a beach sitter? If you can get a friend to go in with you, all the better.

Set up your business at a specific spot on the beach. If there's a distinctive outcropping of rocks or some other landmark, that would be a good place. Have a couple of umbrellas for shade and some sand toys. Make some pretty, bright-colored banners to fly from poles, something to attract attention to your place on the beach. Set up your camp early in the morning and watch as people come down to the beach. When you see a family with little kids, go over and introduce yourselves. Give them a handout which says something like this.

ALICE BECKWITH AND JANE GOZZI
SPECIALISTS IN BEACH BABYSITTING
WE WILL WATCH YOUR CHILD FOR 10 MINUTES
OR SEVERAL HOURS.
$3.00 PER HOUR
WE WILL NOT TAKE CHILDREN IN THE WATER.

You should be at the beach each day at the same time and in the same place so that people will know that they can count on you.

Come prepared. Have a large thermos of water or lemonade, your lunches, and some sort of snacks for the kids. If children are to be left through the lunch hour, make sure that their parents provide a picnic lunch for them.

Bring a supply of good sunscreen. Unless you know for sure that a child has some on, slather the child with it right at the start. You'll be surprised how many parents don't remember to do it. Have a couple of pairs of long pants, a long-sleeved shirt or two, and some hats with wide brims to put on kids who look like they're getting burned.

Most little kids are perfectly happy playing in the sand in their own way, but you might have a few games in mind if they get fussy. Have a quiet place set up under an umbrella with a big beach towel and some books.

Here are some things to remember.

1. Don't take the kids in the water. Bring buckets of it to them.

2. Never let children wander away from your camp or leave them unattended, even for a few minutes.

3. Cover the kids with sunscreen every hour or so (it rubs off).

4. Have some extra clothes to put on a child who's getting sunburned or cold.

5. Since you may not know the people you're sitting for, take a precaution. Give the parents a ticket when they drop off their child. Tell them you won't let the child go with anyone who doesn't give you the ticket. *Be very serious about this.* Most parents will appreciate your care.

Get a name and phone number you can call in case of an emergency.

108

The Saturday Sometimes Puppet Palace

Most kids like shows a whole lot, and if there are loads of little kids in the neighborhood, here is an idea you could think about. You could start a Saturday puppet theater in your garage, backyard, or in a park near your house. Not every Saturday, just sometimes. All you need are puppets, a theater, and a story. Here are some ideas about all three!

~1~
MAKING THE PUPPETS

You've seen hand puppets, the kind you put on the way you do funny gloves, the ones that move when you wiggle your fingers. You can make them easily from odds and ends found around the house. You can use old mittens or socks. You can sew on button eyes and felt mouths and ears. Yarn makes good hair. There are lots of books in the library that tell how to make other kinds of hand puppets.

~2~
MAKING THE PUPPET PALACE

A puppet palace can be a cardboard box, some chairs, and a blanket, or anything that shows the puppets and hides the puppeteer (that's you). Here is a design for one that's easy to make from a big cardboard box (the kind that mattresses and refrigerators and other big things come in). Ask around at a furniture or appliance store for a box. When you get it, here's what you do.

1. Cut open the back and top. You can throw the back away or save it for your background scenery.

2. Cut a simple design in the top, and a hole for the stage in the front wall.

3. Open out the sides so the palace stands up.

109

4. String a wire to the back corners to keep your palace from opening too far.

5. String another wire about a foot from the front and hang your background on it with clothespins. (Make your background bigger than the stage opening.)

6. Paint the palace, or glue pictures all over it, or both.

7. Tape boxes for props to the two side walls. They will add support for your palace.

PUTTING ON THE SHOW

Start out by writing short puppet shows with only a few characters. Try to keep the plots simple and stay away from complicated sets or props. Your audience will be mostly very young kids, and you want them to be able to understand what's going on. After you have rehearsed your show a couple of times and you think it is ready for the public, you need to let people know about it. Several days before you plan to give your show, put up some posters around your neighborhood. Put them up at the library or the playground or at the market. Think of places where people with little kids are apt to go.

Charging admission. At first, don't charge more than 10¢ for kids and 25¢ for adults. Later on, when you have more experience and are writing longer plays, you can charge more.

Toby Wilson's Berry Business

Scout your neighborhood to find where the wild berries grow. You're in business as soon as they get ripe. Many folks are too lazy or too busy to grab a pail and go pick them. They don't know how nice it is to stand outside listening for frogs or crickets and watching for birds or rabbits while they pick. And they don't know how good a ripe berry tastes straight from the bush. If they did, they'd all be there. Toby Wilson (brother of Jon) used to pick wild blueberries. He would pick them by the bucket, then package them in plastic bags and sell them to neighbors for 25¢ per bag.

You could pick blueberries (for muffins and pies, or to go on top of breakfast cereal), huckleberries, blackberries, boysenberries, strawberries—any kind that grows in a place where it's okay to pick. (Don't be like the boy who picked flowers right out of someone's garden and then sold them to all the neighbors.) Be sure you have permission if the berries grow on the neighbor's property.

How to Make a Freezer Berry Bag

TOBY WILSON HAD A SURE FIRE METHOD FOR PUTTING HIS BERRIES IN BAGS. HE USED PLASTIC FREEZER BAGS, WHICH HE FILLED.

THEN HE SUCKED THE AIR OUT OF EACH ONE WITH A STRAW.

THEN HE TIED THE TOPS WITH A TWISTY. HIS METHOD PRESERVES THE BERRIES WELL IN THE FREEZER AND MAKES A NICE NEAT PACKAGE TO SELL.

Freezer-Ready Berries

The Supersandwich Makers

There are a couple of things you should know before you go into this business. To do it you have to like to *eat* sandwiches. Not icky sandwiches, with squishy white bread, limp lunch meat, and presliced cheese that tastes like soap. I mean big, bulging, healthy, munchy, toothsome sandwiches that taste like something real. You've got to like to eat sandwiches like those in order to know how to make them. Next, you have to have a good place to sell your sandwiches, and be pretty certain you can sell them, because in order to start this business, you'll need help from your mother or father or from some other adult. And maybe a loan.

IT WILL TAKE ABOUT $20.00 WORTH OF SUPPLIES TO MAKE TWENTY SANDWICHES LIKE THE ONES WE'RE PROPOSING. SO YOU'LL NEED $20.00 TO GET STARTED IN BUS-INESS. (THE MONEY YOU USE TO GET STARTED IS CALLED "CAPITAL.") BUT IF YOU SELL TWENTY SUPERSAND-WICHES FOR $2.00 EACH, YOU'LL GET YOUR $20.00 BACK AND HAVE $20.00 LEFTOVER. NOT BAD FOR A MORNING'S WORK.

How to start in business if you don't have $20.00. Go to the neighborhood market and tell the owner your plan. Tell him you want to sweep, or wash windows, or deliver groceries, or go around the neighborhood collecting stray grocery carts to raise $20.00 to spend at his store. If he is any kind of a businessman, he'll understand what you are trying to do and help you. (He might even let you sell sandwiches at the store.) Or you could tell your mom or dad or other adult that you'll wash windows, mow lawns, or do other chores to raise the money. Or, as a last resort, take out a loan. Just remember, if you borrow $20.00 to start your business, you should be prepared to pay "interest" on the money. That means that when you pay back the loan, you pay back the $20.00 plus something extra for the use of the money.

Now, about the sandwiches. Here are four super-sandwich recipes. (Don't try to make too many kinds. Three or four kinds are plenty.) Try these, and add your own recipes until you find out which ones sell best.

The Cheese Special

SPREAD MAYONNAISE ON TWO SLICES OF GOOD, SOLID WHOLE WHEAT BREAD. HEAP ON A GENEROUS PORTION OF FRESHLY GRATED, AGED CHEDDAR CHEESE. ADD THIN SLICES OF TOMATO, AVOCADO AND RED ONION.

(THEY'LL SAY, "GIMME CHEESE, PLEASE!")

The Cream Cheese Sweet

MASH A LARGE PACKAGE (12 OUNCES) OF CREAM CHEESE UNTIL IT'S VERY SMOOTH. ADD CHOPPED, DRIED APRICOTS; RAISINS; OR OTHER DRIED FRUIT. SPREAD IT ON RAISIN-NUT BREAD. (YOU CAN WRAP THESE IN HALVES AND SELL THEM AS A KIND OF DESSERT FOR $1.00 EACH.)

THIS RECIPE MAKES FOUR WHOLE SANDWICHES.

The Egg-Salad Wonder

HARD-BOIL ONE EGG FOR EACH SANDWICH. REMOVE THE SHELL AND CHOP THE EGG UP FINELY. MIX WITH MAYONNAISE, CHOPPED ALMONDS, AND GREEN ONION SLICES. SPREAD THICKLY ON RYE BREAD.

The Cottage Cheese Crunch

MIX A 16-OUNCE CARTON OF COTTAGE CHEESE WITH A HANDFUL OF SHELLED AND SALTED SUNFLOWER SEEDS AND A HALF CUP OF CUCUMBER CHOPPED INTO TINY PIECES. SPREAD ON WHOLE WHEAT BREAD, ADD A LITTLE SALT, THIN ONION SLICES, AND ALFALFA SPROUTS.

THIS RECIPE MAKES SIX SANDWICHES.

Making your sandwiches. Make your sandwiches right after breakfast each day. You may want to boil the eggs the night before, but the other stuff will taste better if it's prepared the same day. *Never* try to make the sandwiches the night before.

Arrange things so that you can put all the cheese sandwiches together at once, then all the egg sandwiches, and so on. If you have a helper, you can divide up the work. Wrap the sandwiches in waxed paper or clear plastic and tie them with colored yarn. The yarn looks nice, and you can use the colors to help you tell egg from cheese. Charge $2.00 per sandwich. Make a sign to go with your sandwiches. The sign should say something like this.

**HAVE A
SUPERSANDWICH
MADE FRESH THIS MORNING
IN MOM'S KITCHEN BY
MORRIS AND MARTHA
$2.00 EACH
YOU'LL WISH YOU'D BOUGHT TWO!**

Where to sell sandwiches. If you can get permission, go around to offices near your house. Especially go to places where people would go out and buy their lunches anyway. (Tell them it's such a nice day, they ought to eat a sandwich outdoors.) Be sure to get started selling early, at least by ten o'clock. No one will be interested in sandwiches in the afternoon. Until you have established a number of places to go and have a good idea of how many you can sell, don't make too many sandwiches. It is better to sell out than to have leftovers. Start with a Monday–Wednesday–Friday schedule, rather than every day. (You may need some days in between to go swimming.)

113

The Great Indianapolis Trike Track

Little kids like to pretend that their tricycles are cars. You and your friends could set up a great trike track in a local playground or an unused parking lot, where kids could pretend to their hearts' content.

Here's how to do it

You'll need a large paved area that's off-limits to automobiles. It is best if the area is fenced. Get a bunch of your friends together to plot it out. Draw a rough plan of the area and a design for the tricycle roadway. Just like professional road planners, you'll have to think about the flow of traffic and safety. Avoid making dangerous intersections or hazards, but make the track as interesting and as varied as you can.

Some things to make

At the entrance, where you sell tickets, charge each child 25¢ and give him or her a book of tickets. It can be little slips of paper stapled together in batches of twenty. There should be a tollbooth with a toll taker who demands one ticket as soon as the kids enter the track. Don't admit any kid who is too big to ride a tricycle sitting down.

The road should be *one-way only* to avoid head-on collisions. (You can reverse the direction occasionally to make things more interesting.) Mark the roadway with chalk or with scrap lumber. Have stop signs and a speed limit. Make many curves and turns.

If the road crosses itself, have a "policeman" at the intersection to direct traffic. She should have a whistle and a big stop sign to hold.

One of you should act as a highway patrolman. Wear a uniform. Stand on the back step of a tricycle and push yourself around with your foot. (A scooter, too, would make a good patrol car.) Have a jail where you take people who don't obey the traffic laws. Fine them one ticket and let them go quickly.

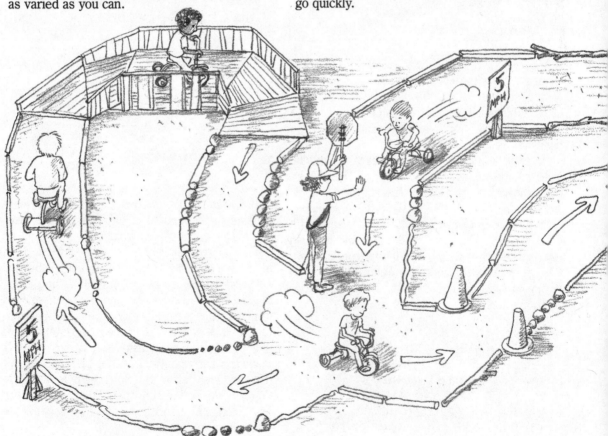

Make a tunnel from big cardboard cartons (like the ones mattresses come in). It should be high enough for the kids to ride through without ducking. Have a tollbooth at the entrance and take another ticket.

Make a bridge with a low ramp (no more than a foot high) and railings. Don't make a bridge unless you have plenty of lumber to work with so you can make it very sturdy and wide enough to be safe.

Have some places where there is road work going on. Put out orange cones and have everyone slow down. Make the cones out of cardboard and paint them bright orange.

Have an exit road from the first tollbooth. When kids have run out of tickets, they will have to go out and pay another entrance fee. The kids should be able to get ten rounds from one book of tickets, unless they're very reckless and get arrested too many times.

You'll be able to dream up lots more ideas for your trike track. Remember to think about safety first. Enforce the speed limit and remove any child who gets too wild to handle (even if you have to refund the child's money).

Advertising

Start about a week before the event. Tell people in your neighborhood who have little kids all about it. Explain what you are going to do to make it safe and fun. Put up posters in places where little kids are apt to go with their parents.

The Big Block Fair

Set up an advertising committee of two or three kids. Make banners, posters, and flyers to hang and pass around the neighborhood and nearby neighborhoods a couple of weeks before the fair. Another good idea is to select a symbol or logo for the fair. Example: if the fair is being held on Oak Avenue, the oak leaf would make a good symbol. Put this symbol on all your posters. This kind of advertisement will help people remember the fair. Make name tags for the fair workers so people will recognize them and know whom to ask if they have any questions about the fair.

This neighborhood event could be the grand finale of a summer spent making cents. Here's a way to celebrate the many ways of having fun, making money, and getting to know all the folks in your neighborhood.

You and a few friends can be the organizers of this event. Talk to your friends about the idea; talk to your parents. When everyone is excited about the idea, it's time to set the date, place, and time. If you plan to have it on your block, you might have to discuss closing the street with your local police department or town council. Most likely they'll get into the spirit and say yes.

The fair organizers will have to decide how many booths and events to have. Make sure there is a lot of variety: you don't want to end up with five booths selling cookies. You'll need one person who signs up the people who want to have booths. Draw a diagram of the block and mark on it the location of each booth or table and record the person's name as each booth is reserved. Assign a number, so there will be no confusion on fair day. On the morning of the fair, someone should take a piece of chalk and mark the numbers on the pavement so when people arrive they know exactly where to go. All people who participate should make their own booths or bring their own tables.

Here are some ideas for the fair.

1. Set up an easel and do quickie portraits with felt-tipped pens. Charge 25¢ per drawing.

2. Make a sandwich-board sign that says: I love to babysit. Call Lael, 383-5768.

3. Set up a Garden of Delight. Sell plants, packets of seeds, dried flowers, and small pots of fragrant herbs.

4. Present a Three-Penny Opera. Train your dog to howl (hound dogs do this best). Howl with him. Wear tattered clothes and tie a bandanna around your dog's neck. This spectacle will be worth three pennies, maybe more.

5. Display and sell all the craft items you've been making all summer: candles, printed cards, stuffed animals, pincushions, hats, and toys.

6. Form a jug or kazoo band. Wear funny get-ups. Pass a hat after each performance.

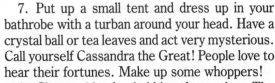

7. Put up a small tent and dress up in your bathrobe with a turban around your head. Have a crystal ball or tea leaves and act very mysterious. Call yourself Cassandra the Great! People love to hear their fortunes. Make up some whoppers!

8. Charge 10¢ for bobbing for apples. The prize for winning is a juicy apple to eat. Nonwinners get a clean face.

9. Paint a funny scene on a large piece of cardboard. Have holes in the right places for people's heads. Take their pictures with a Polaroid camera and charge $2.00 per picture. (They will cost you about $1.20.) If people have their own cameras, charge them 25¢ for using the backdrop.

10. Be the good-food kid. Sell homemade sandwiches and lemonade. You'll have the busiest booth at the fair.

11. Gather up all the good junk you've been collecting and set up a flea market stall. Sell repaired toys, records, books, and eucalyptus-pod flea collars.

12. Decorate a cardboard box and make raffle tickets. Sell the tickets for 20¢ each. The winner of this event gets two hours of free babysitting from you. You might come out ahead on this, and you'll get a lot of free advertisement for your service.

13. Present a rollicking puppet show with puppets you've made. Make a simple theater out of a large cardboard box. Charge 10¢ for admission. If you make a lot of puppets, you could sell them after the show for $1.00 each. Hand out flyers offering to give puppet shows at birthday parties.

14. Everybody loves balloons filled with helium. Get a tank of helium (you'll need a grownup to help) and a good supply of balloons. You fill them while a couple of your friends stroll around the fair selling them.

15. Set up a game-of-chance booth. Pitch pennies into saucers. (It's harder than it looks.) Give a piece of hard candy for each penny that stays in a saucer. You get to keep all the pennies that miss. Start with a good supply of pennies for making change.

16. Make a shooting-star beanbag toss. Cut some moon, sun, and star shapes out of a big piece of cardboard. Give each hole a value, the smallest having the highest value. Give people five throws for 25¢. People who score 200 or more get a prize. The prizes could be giant star cookies. Have plenty of extra shooting-star beanbags to sell at 50¢ each.

You and Your Money

The last few pages of this book look quite different from the rest of the book. There are fewer drawings and no ideas for making money, but I think you may find them interesting just the same. Until now all we have talked about is how to make money. We haven't talked about money itself or how it came to be or what happens to it after you've earned it or a number of other interesting subjects.

In these Green Pages (green because that's the color of money) we will talk a little about some of those things, about banks and how to put your money in them and how to get it out. We'll talk about income taxes and Social Security cards and licenses and permits, things that you probably won't have to deal with until you're a little older, but good things to know about anyway.

The Green Pages also talk about some things that will be very important to you right now! Things like how to keep track of the money you earn and, if you have partners in your business, how to make sure everyone gets a fair share of the profits. They tell you how to make change without getting confused and how to decide what business to go into in the first place.

One of the most important parts of The Green Pages is about the things you can do to make your customers happy and to ensure that they will want to do business with you again and again.

What Is Money?

Money is something that almost everyone would like to have lots of. Most people spend a good deal of their time thinking and worrying about whether they have enough and how to get more. You hear a lot of nonsense being spouted about money. You probably know people who talk about how terrible it is to want money and how unimportant it is and about how *they* don't care a thing about money. Don't be fooled; they're prob-

ably people who have never been without money in their lives. The fact is that without money we would all be in a terrible mess.

Money isn't *dirty* or *wonderful* or *magic*; it's really just a convenient device that makes it easier for us to trade one thing for another. Before the invention of money as we know it, people used various things in its place. The earliest method of getting things that you needed was through barter, that is, trading something you had for something someone else had. It wasn't always a convenient method. Let's say you made shoes and I grew prunes. If I happened to need a pair of shoes and you wanted a bushel of prunes, that would have been great. But what would you do if I didn't need shoes? You'd have to search all over for someone who wanted your shoes and who had something that I wanted to trade for my prunes. It would get much too complicated. Barter really works only in societies where people's needs are very simple and predictable.

In most early civilizations, some one or two things came to be used very much like money. Sometimes they were useful items such as tools, salt, slaves, or domesticated animals. In other places, some very strange things like feathers, round stones, or human skulls were used in much the same way. All of these were things that could be accumulated and traded for labor or goods.

With the coming of the Bronze Age (about 3000 B.C.), bronze became the major medium of exchange. It could be stockpiled in the form of crude bars or fabricated into weapons, tools, or ornaments and had value throughout the civilized world.

The first actual money was made in the form of coins. They were made of gold, silver, or electrum (a combination of the two). In the seventh century B.C., Greek city-states issued coins with a standard value, and by the time of Alexander the Great the Greek drachma was the commonly accepted money in every Mediterranean country and as far away as India. There was one major problem with the use of gold and silver coins, and that was that there was no guarantee of their value. Of course, dishonest rulers and governments soon started to debase their coins (put in less gold or silver and add more common metals) or clip and shave bits off so they could make more coins. This problem was never really solved as long as coins containing precious metals were in circulation.

Our coins today have *no* precious metal in them at all, and, of course, neither does our paper money. Originally, these coins and bills were backed by gold or silver; that is, the government held enough of these precious metals so that anyone who wished could turn in bills or coins for an equal value of gold or silver. This is no longer true. Our currency is now only partially backed by gold, and you cannot redeem it for gold or silver. So why is our money worth something? Well, the best answer I can find for that is it's worth something because most people think it is. People will take it in exchange for goods or labor because they are sure that they, in turn, can buy goods and labor with it. When you come to think about it, money is a pretty peculiar thing, and maybe it really is a sort of magic!

You and the Bank

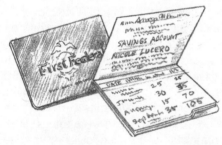

If you earn a little money now and then, and you don't have any plans for spending it right away, it is probably a good idea to open a savings account at a bank near you. Each bank has different rules about what kids can do, so check out the bank you choose before you decide to put your money there.

If you are eighteen or older and have a driver's license, you can open your own savings and checking accounts just about anywhere. If you are under eighteen, *some* banks will allow you to open a savings account in your own name. One

bank I checked has what is called a "student savings account," which is for anyone who is a student and under twenty-one. You can both open the account and withdraw money from it without an adult signature. Another bank will allow only what is called a "trust account" in conjunction with a parent or guardian. This is a polite way of saying that the bank prefers not to let kids be responsible for their own money. The parent or guardian must sign the application card and must sign each time the child takes out money. (Anyone can deposit money.)

When you put money into a savings account, the bank pays you "interest" if you leave it there for three months or more. Interest is a payment of a certain percentage of the amount of money you have in the account. The percentage of interest paid depends on which bank you go to. You may wonder how the bank can afford to pay you for keeping your money. It's because the bank makes a profit on it. The bank doesn't simply put your money in the safe and let it sit there. The bank puts it to work. One way the bank puts your money to work is by lending it to other people. Say, for example, a young man wants to start a business or buy a house. He probably doesn't have enough money to pay for it all at once, so he asks the bank to lend him some money and promises to pay it back within a certain time. He also agrees to pay the bank some extra money (interest) as well. In other words, the person who borrows pays for the use of the money. The bank in turn pays you for using your money.

A "checking account" is a different story. Most banks will not let you open a checking account until you are over eighteen and have a driver's license. With a checking account the bank holds your money and allows you to pay for things by writing a check rather than by giving someone cash money. You don't have to carry the money around and risk losing it, and you can safely send a check through the mail. Whomever you make the check out to then gets the money from the bank or deposits the check directly into his or her own account, and the banks take care of the exchange. The bank charges you a fee for this service unless you keep a good deal of money in your account. Some checking accounts pay interest just like savings accounts do, but you must keep a certain amount of money (balance) in the account at all times.

Most banks will let you open a "joint checking account" with a parent or guardian, but the adult must sign every check along with you (cosign). This is because it is very easy to get confused about how much money you have in your account. Lots of grown-ups mess up their checking accounts, so the banks probably figure that kids would get even more confused. For example, say I have $300.00 in my checking account. I write a check for $59.00 to pay my gas and electric bill, but the phone rings just as I put it in the envelope. I answer the phone and forget to write the amount in my checkbook. That's okay today because I've got plenty of money in the bank to pay the bill. I write a couple of other small checks for groceries and dry cleaning. Then my car breaks down, and I take it to the garage for repairs. The bill comes to $230.00. I look in my checkbook and think, Great, I have just enough to pay for my car! I write a check and drive off. In a few days I get an angry phone call from the mechanic. He tells me that my check has "bounced" (my bank sent it back because I didn't have enough money in my account). My bank calls to tell me I've overdrawn my account and there will be an extra charge because of the extra paperwork involved. As you can see, it's very easy to lose track, and the bank has pretty good reasons for its rules about kids' checking accounts.

It will probably be a while before you really need a checking account anyway, but it's a good idea to know something about the whole business. To put money into a checking account, you need a "deposit slip." When you open a checking account, the bank will issue you a book of personalized checks (with your name and account number already printed on them). In the back of the book of checks, there will be some personalized deposit slips as well. They are preprinted with your name, bank branch, and account number. The deposit slips will look something like this.

You write the amount of money you are putting into your account on the deposit slip. Notice that there is a space for currency (paper money) and a space for coins. Then there are several spaces where you enter checks, which are always listed separately by amount. If you have more than two or three checks to deposit, use the back of the deposit slip, which has thirteen more spaces. Add them all together to get your total deposit. You must then endorse your checks by writing your name on the back of each one. Under your name write "for deposit only" and your account number. This is a safety measure to keep someone else from cashing your checks. Then take your deposit slip, checks, and cash to the teller at the bank. The teller will check your figures and give you a receipt to show how much money has been deposited in your account.

If you want to take money out of your checking account or pay a bill, you will have to write a check. A personalized check has your name and your cosigner's name and address, the name and branch address of the bank, your account number, and a branch code number printed on the face of the check. Each check in the book will be numbered in consecutive order. You must write

121

the name of the business or person to whom the money is to be paid, the date, the amount, and your signature. Then if it is a joint account, you must have it cosigned by your parent or guardian.

When you get your checkbook, the bank will give you another book, called a "check register." This is where you keep track of your money. As you make deposits into your account, you make a notation in your check register. You write where the money came from, the date, and the amount. Whenever you write a check, you make a note of it in the check register. You write the number of the check, the date, to whom it was paid, and the amount. On the right-hand side of the register, you keep a running total of your balance. You add in your deposits as you make them and subtract your checks as you write them. When you first have a checking account, it is probably a good idea to do this after each transaction. Later on, when you have more money in the bank and have gotten used to keeping within your budget, you may decide that you need to total up only once a week or once a month, when you get your bank statement.

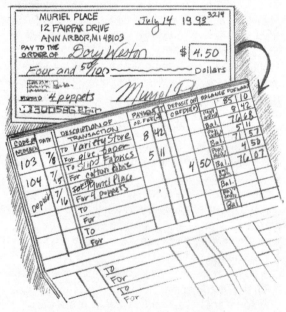

Once a month the bank sends you a "statement," a record of what has happened in your account (both checking and savings). The bank also sends you back all of your checks that have been cashed. The statement tells you the date and amount of each deposit; the number, date, and amount of each check you wrote (if it has been

cashed); any service charges made by the bank that have been deducted from your account; and any interest that has been added to your account. When you receive the statement, you have the opportunity to check up on the bank. Go through your records and match them to the bank's records. If you think that the bank has made a mistake, this is the time to straighten it out. Most often, you'll find that you made a simple mistake in addition or subtraction, but occasionally the bank is wrong, so be sure to satisfy yourself about any discrepancies.

You and the Government

One of the ways that both state and federal governments earn money to stay in business is by collecting taxes from people. Anyone who makes more than a certain amount in a single year must pay income tax to the federal government on April 15 of the following year. Most state governments collect income taxes too. They collect it on the same day the federal taxes are paid. (Actually, you mail it to them.)

The magic figure is $2,540. If you earn even one dollar more than that amount in one year, you must file a tax return and pay some tax. (The magic number changes from time to time. It used to be $600.) Most kids will not earn that much money until they get regular jobs. But it's possible to earn that much, so you might as well know about income tax rules.

If you are under eighteen and living at home, you are considered to be "dependent" on your parents no matter how much money you make yourself. So even if you make over $2,540 on your own, you must pay federal income tax, and—depending on where you live—maybe state income tax too.

Both state and federal governments have offices in big cities. Look in the white pages of your telephone book under "United States Government" or the name of your state. The agency that collects federal income tax is called the Internal Revenue Service. For the states, the name varies. In California it's called the State of California Franchise Tax Board. In your state it might be something else. You'll just have to ask.

There is another governmental agency you need to know about. It's called the Social Security Administration. It is the agency that pays some money to people every month when they get old enough to retire. It functions like a big lifetime savings account. A certain part of your income is paid into that account each time you pay income taxes. Then when you reach the age of sixty-two, you can apply to draw on that money. How much you get each month depends on how much money you made while you were paying into the account.

Each person who works gets a card from the Social Security Administration, and we keep that card all of our lives. It has a number on it, which is how the government keeps track of each person's money. Here is what one looks like.

The number at the top is the account number. In order to file an income tax return, you'll need to have a Social Security card like this one, with your own account number.

Everybody must apply for a Social Security card. The law now requires all five-year-olds to have one. It costs nothing. All you have to do is fill out a simple form and sign your name. You will be required to show a copy of your birth certificate when you apply, so ask your parents to provide yours. To find out where to apply for your Social Security card, look in the white pages of your phone book under "United States Government" and then under "Social Security Administration." Most big cities have an office. You can get a card by mail too.

Permits and Licenses

Most businesses that are run by adults are, in one way or another, regulated by some part of the government. Most regulation is intended to protect customers: some is intended to provide taxes, which pay for running the government.

The regulation takes the form of permits or licenses (or both) and taxes. Until you are of legal age (which in most states is eighteen), you probably won't have to think much about regulations. They are a tricky business. In most places, kids are permitted to do their work without having to bother with them.

But if you spend very much of your time doing work, and if that work brings you to the attention of the local governmental officials who enforce regulations, you may have to think about it sooner rather than later.

If that happens, take our advice and discuss the situation with a grown-up. The chances are that whatever regulation is staring you in the face wasn't intended for kids and can be avoided. If it can't, you'll need the assistance of an adult anyway, since most governmental agencies do not recognize the rights and abilities of kids to act for themselves in such matters.

Here are some of the kinds of permits and licenses that are the most common. Since regulations are different in different places, it is not possible to tell which of these are used where you live.

Business license. Usually issued by cities, towns, or counties to anyone who takes money for things they sell. Sometimes there is a small fee for the license.

Food and beverage license. People who sell things to eat are usually required to have a license from the Health Department. You don't need one for a lemonade stand, or for selling cookies or candy door-to-door.

Sales tax license. Regular businesses that sell

anything but food usually charge sales tax. The sales tax, which is a certain percentage of the cost of the item sold, is collected from the buyer and then paid to the city and/or state. That's how governments make part of their money. In order to collect sales tax from customers, you must have a license to do so, and you must keep very careful records of all of your sales. Luckily, this is something you won't have to worry about unless you go into business in a big way.

Keeping Track of Your Money

Even if no one asks you to do it, it's a good idea to keep records. It's one way of knowing where your money is (or was). And it's the only way of knowing for sure whether you are making money or losing it.

What we mean by keeping records is knowing how much money you have earned and how much you have spent. If you have to spend $5.00 in order to earn $3.00, you're not doing very well. Or, rather, you're not doing very well as far as making money is concerned. You might spend $5.00 to put on a neighborhood circus and earn only $3.00 but have so much fun doing it that you don't care about losing $2.00. There's nothing wrong with that just as long as you know about it and can afford it.

Before you can know whether you're making or losing money, you have to set up a system for keeping track of what is being spent and what is being earned. If there is more than one person involved in the business, keeping track is even more important. When two or more people are in business together, you have to keep careful records to make sure that each person pays a fair share of the expenses and gets a fair share of the profits.

Here is a way to keep simple records. You can use this method or invent your own. The principle is the same, no matter how you go about it: Money received (income) less money spent (expenses) leaves money earned (profit or loss).

The cigar-box method. You'll need a cigar box (or some other small, sturdy container) and a bunch of little slips of paper about 2 by 3 inches, some small envelopes, some rubber bands or paper clips, and a pencil.

With this method, you don't keep your money in a bank; you keep it in a cigar box. This means you have to be careful to leave it in a safe place.

This method will work whether there is just one person or several people in business, but it will only work if everybody cooperates. When you spend money, you take it out of the box and write out a receipt on one of the little slips of paper. Every time. You can't skip even one! Each slip of paper should have the following information on it: who took the money, on what day, and what for. When you put money into the box, you enter the amount, the date, and where the money came from on the front of one of the envelopes, like this.

At the end of each week, or, if you like, at the end of each month, you add up all the amounts written down on the front of the envelope and total them. Then you add up all the amounts written on the little slips of paper and deduct the total from the amount on the envelope.

The difference should be equal to the amount left in the box. If there is *more* money in the box, it means that someone forgot to write some income on the envelope. If there is *less* money in the box, it means someone forgot to fill out a little slip when taking money out. (Guess which one happens most often.)

After that, you should put a paper clip or rubber band on all the little slips for the week (or month) and put them into the envelope. If there is more than one person involved, divide up the profits equally and each put a small amount back in the box for any expenses that may come up early in the next week or month.

How to Make Change

What do you do when someone gives you a dollar bill to pay for something that costs 10¢? Do you keep the dollar and say, "Thanks very much"? Do you give it back and say, "That's too much, thanks anyway"? No. You make change, and here's how you do it. All you have to know is how to add.

You have just sold an apple to a football fan. The apple costs 10¢. The fan gives you a dollar bill. The football game is about to start. She is in a hurry. What do you do?

Start with the cost of the apple. Say, "10¢." Then give her the change, coin by coin, and add the coins out loud until you have added up to a dollar. So you would continue, "20¢," (you give her a dime); "25¢," (you give her a nickel); "50¢," (you give her a quarter); "$1.00. Thank you." (you give her a half-dollar).

And that's it. Check and see if that's right.

A dime, a quarter, a nickel, and a half-dollar add up to 90¢. Right?

Now practice with your mom or dad or anyone who can check to make sure you're correct. Do it at least ten times with different amounts until you can do it without having to go back and start over.

Deciding on a Business

Before you decide on the kind of business to go into, it's often a good idea to do a little "market research." That means trying to figure out ahead of time if there are enough people around who might want to buy what you want to sell. How do you find out? Just good common sense and some serious thinking will answer some questions. You'll have no problem figuring out that you won't get many customers for fishing worms if there's no place nearby to fish. But other questions aren't always so obvious, especially if you have just moved into a town or if you don't know your neighbors very well.

The first information on job possibilities should come from your own eyes and ears. Walk around your neighborhood several times on weekends and on weekdays and at different times of day. Listen, look, and take notes. Here are some of the things to notice and write down. Are there:

1. Older people who live by themselves?
2. Families with young children (one parent or two)?
3. People who are away all day at work?
4. Lots of kids around (what ages)?
5. Lawns and gardens (well kept or not)?
6. Mostly houses, or apartments?
7. Houses with For Sale signs (occupied or not)?
8. Businesses and office buildings?

9. Schools and day-care centers?
10. Churches, clubs, and recreation centers?
11. Stores and restaurants?

Once you have all this information, you are in a much better position to decide on which business to go into as well as how to advertise it. For instance, if you are thinking about starting a yardwork or cleanup business, you would know that there are people in the area who might well be interested in your servies. Older people who need help with lifting or digging or people who have only weekends for chores are good bets. Houses for sale might be a source of business. Yards may need sprucing up so they'll be more attractive to potential buyers, or garages and basements may need cleaning out. If you know that there is a senior citizens' center in the neighborhood, you could post a notice on the bulletin board there advertising your service. Real estate offices in the area may have empty houses that need lawn care. If you already know that the potential customers are there, you will have a much better chance of success in whatever you start.

Another type of market research is to find out who you would have to compete with. Say, for example, you were thinking about going into the sandwich business. You already know that there is a big office complex within a few blocks of your house and that many of the people who work there like to sit outdoors and eat their lunches. Check out the restaurants in the area that have take-out service. They would be your competition. See how much they charge for their sandwiches, what the sandwiches look like, and what sorts of things they put in them. Then, armed with that information, you can plan your attack. Make your sandwiches bigger, healthier, more appetizing, and, if you can and still make money, less expensive. You should have lots of happy customers in a very short time.

Sometimes the most direct way to find out about your market is by doing a survey. Think about a whole bunch of jobs that you might want to do. Make up a list of them and go out ringing doorbells. You should probably do this on a weekend, when people are most likely to be home. Introduce yourself and tell them where you live. Tell them right away that you're taking a survey so they don't think you're selling magazines or raffle tickets. Tell them that you are thinking about going into business and that you are trying to find out what sort of jobs people most often want done. Mark down what they say. At the end ask what job *they* hate doing the most. This may give you an idea for a business that you hadn't thought about. Tally up the answers and decide which type of work is in the greatest demand. Then distribute a flyer to all the people you surveyed announcing the results and the opening of your new business. The survey will have several effects. It gives you a better idea of what people want, it introduces you to your prospective customers, and it makes them feel as if they had some part in starting your business, all of which can only help you.

Another type of market research is the free sample. Big companies use it all the time. It's really more of an advertising gimmick than true market research, but it works very well and could work for you too. Of course, you couldn't afford to give away free samples of something that cost a lot or that took a long time to make, but there are some things that lend themselves to this technique.

If you were interested in going into the cookie business, you could make several batches of very small cookies, wrap them in some clever way, and attach them to a questionaire. Ask people to fill out the questionnaire and tell them you will collect it the next day. Put your name and telephone number on it, as well as some information about yourself. Tell how old you are and about your idea for starting a cookie business. Ask if they liked the cookie, if they would buy cookies like the sample, and how much they would pay for a dozen of them. Ask if there is any other kind of cookie they would prefer.

It's possible to give free samples of a service as well. Truly, this is much more like advertising than like market research, though it might provide you with some important information. If you were interested in babysitting jobs, you could make up a flyer telling about yourself and how much you charge. You could include some names of happy customers (get their permission to do this beforehand). On the bottom corner, have a coupon good for 30 minutes of free daytime babysitting. Be sure to include your telephone number and the hours you are free. The 30-minute trial is a good way for people to get an idea of your babysitting skills and for you to find out something about the child and the adults you would be babysitting for. Be prepared with a short puppet show or an exciting story to break the ice.

Here are some other ideas for free samples. If you're in the window-washing business, offer to wash one window free. (It might be smart to make a size restriction on the window.) If you're starting a neighborhood newspaper, give out a free copy with a questionnaire asking people if they'd be interested in getting it once a week, or however often you think you would like to publish it.

Business Ethics

I'm sure you know what ethics are. You and your parents have talked about them since you were very little, but you may not have called them by that name. Ethics are the rules you make for yourself about how to behave and about how you treat other people. How are business ethics different from just plain everyday ethics? Well, they aren't really different, but talking about them may help you to think about the question in a different way than you have before. For instance, you know that when you do something that breaks the rules you and your family have worked out, you may be punished and may well lose some privileges for a while, but you also know that your family still loves you and forgives you. If you break the rules in business, you often don't get another chance. You not only lose your customers, but it leaves you with a bad feeling about yourself.

What are some of the ethics you already know about? Honesty, to begin with. When you are working for people and are in or around their house, you must never forget that what belongs to them is theirs, including their privacy. Don't peek in drawers, read letters, or look in places where you have no business to be. You would hate it if someone snooped around in your room without your permission, so don't do it to others. Don't discuss anything private that you may have heard or seen in your customer's house with anyone else unless it's something that worries you. Then talk about it only with your parents or some other adult whom you trust.

Of course, you wouldn't dream of taking anything in someone else's house, but in business, it's a good idea to take honesty one step further, that is, to make sure that your customer knows that you wouldn't. If you're babysitting and think that you may get hungry, ask beforehand if there is something in the house you can eat. Or if there's something left out that you're quite sure was meant for you, it's still a good idea to tell your customer that you ate it and that you hope it was okay.

If you break or damage something while you're doing a job, don't try to hide it or deny it. Tell your customer immediately. He may be mad at the moment, but not half as mad as if he found out later.

Be trustworthy and reliable! Don't tell people you'll do something or be someplace at a certain hour and then not do it. If you are gong to be late and cannot help it, *call your customers*, and tell them why you're not there and when you will be able to come. If something happens and you can't make an appointment and can't call to tell them, at the first opportunity, go in person to apologize and explain.

If you are doing a job that pays by the hour, be sure that you keep accurate records. Don't count

127

time that you spend just goofing off; count only the time that you are actually working.

Anyone who has a job soon figures out that there are all sorts of way to cut corners and to get something that you haven't worked for. Some people go through life doing that. You may think that these people are getting away with it and that nobody knows about their dishonesty, but you would be wrong. They do get caught. Employers learn to spot them in a hurry and get rid of them as fast as they can. But worst of all, they get caught in their own discontent and unhappiness. They're the people who are always complaining about being treated badly, about having to work too hard, and about how other people have all the luck.

The other kind of people are the ones who always do a little more than people expect them to, who are enthusiastic and cheerful about their work, and who are careful about their hours and charges. They are the people employers brag about and recommend to their friends. They are the ones who have fun doing the job and feel good about the money they earn.

Looking Out for Yourself

We've been talking about the things you should do for your customers; now let's talk about the things you should do for yourself. There's an old saying: The customer is always right. Well, that's usually a good rule, but there are times when it's not. Chances are you'll never run into a customer who is wrong, but if you do, you should have some idea about how to protect yourself.

1. If you are working in someone's house and that person starts to say things that frighten you or make you uncomfortable or if the person touches you in a way you don't like, get out of the house immediately. Don't worry about leaving tools or possessions, just go as fast as you can. Tell your parents or some other adult *immediately*. Give them as accurate an account of what happened or of what was said as you can. If you go back for your possessions, have an adult go with you.

2. Sometimes customers say they don't have change, or some such thing, and can't pay you right away. This may be the truth, and they may pay you later. But if it happens more than once with the same customer, don't just let it go. You are entitled to be paid immediately for work you have done. Be polite, but ask when the customer will have the money and offer to come around to collect it. If that doesn't work, write a note saying that you need the money and that you will come the next day to collect it. Enclose a bill for your work. The next time that customer wants you to work, say that you're busy. (That's not a lie, because you'll be busy looking for customers who will pay you on time.)

3. If a customer asks you to do something dangerous, such as climb out on a roof to wash upstairs windows or climb up a wobbly ladder, just say that you won't. Say that your parents told you not to or that you get dizzy. Or just say plainly that it's dangerous and that you don't wish to do it, and stick to your guns.

4. If you are taking care of a child who behaves very badly, let the parents know that you had trouble. Don't assume that it is all your fault and go on putting up with it. And don't pretend that everything went well. Tell the parents what happened and ask if they have any ideas about how you can keep it from happening again. They might have a suggestion that will help you be a better babysitter, or they might not know that their child acts awful when they're not around. Don't say that Suzy was a monster (even if she was). Say that you didn't seem to be able to make Suzy mind. That way you can let them know what their child misbehaved without sounding too critical. If you can't solve the problem, politely decline any further babysitting jobs with them. You and the child should both enjoy your time together, and if you don't, it's not a good arrangement for either of you.